FAMILY CHANGE AND HOUSING IN POST-WAR JAPANESE SOCIETY

Family Change and Housing in Post-War Japanese Society

The experiences of older women

MISA IZUHARA
School for Policy Studies
Universty of Bristol

Ashgate

Aldershot • Burlington USA • Singapore • Sydney

Published by
Ashgate Publishing Ltd
Gower House
Croft Road
Aldershot
Hants GU11 3HR
England

Ashgate Publishing Company
131 Main Street
Burlington
Vermont 05401
USA

Ashgate website: http://www.ashgate.com

British Library Cataloguing in Publication Data
Izuhara, Misa
    Family change and housing in post-war Japanese society :
    the experiences of older women
    1.Aged women - Japan - Social conditions 2.Aged women -
    Housing - Japan 3.Family - Japan 4.Japan - Social
    conditions - 1945-
    I.Title
    305.2'6'0952'09045

Library of Congress Catalog Card Number: 00-132596

ISBN 0 7546 1284 8

Printed in Great Britain by
Antony Rowe Ltd, Chippenham, Wiltshire

Contents

List of Figures and Tables

Acknowledgments

I would like to take this opportunity to express my gratitude to Professor Ray Forrest for his academic advice, support and encouragement throughout my research work. It is impossible to identify and acknowledge all those individuals and organizations who provided information, time, support and inspiration during my research in both England and Japan. I want to thank especially those older women who contributed positively and enthusiastically to my fieldwork. My appreciation has to go to my family in Japan, especially my mother for her never-ending support and patience, and also Simon, my great editor. The interpretation of the data and views expressed in this book are entirely those of the author.

1 Introduction

The world is growing older. The proportion of older people is growing, much faster than the global population as a whole. By the year 2000, this growth rate will result in more than 410 million older people world-wide (41% and 59% in developed and developing countries, respectively), compared with 290 million in 1987 (46% and 54%, respectively) (US Bureau of the Census, 1987). In most developed societies, one of the most significant and emerging demographic facts affecting the current and future course of societal development is the ageing of the population. The ratio of 'societal ageing' (the percentage of 'older people'[1] in the total population) increased rapidly while population growth slowed during the 20th century. In line with these trends, Japan has also experienced significant changes in its age structure, and is now at the forefront of an ageing world.

Since 1950, fertility has decreased very sharply, and now Japan has one of the lowest birth-rates in the world (1.43[2] in the mid-1990s). This low birth-rate, combined with reductions in infant and maternal mortality, and an increase in life expectancy (82.8 years for females, 76.4 years for males in 1995), has brought about a very sharp increase in the number and proportion of the older population (Maeda, 1993).   This tendency is expected to continue until the beginning of the twenty-first century, when the rates of societal ageing in Japan will become one of the highest in the world (US Bureau of the Census, 1993) (Table 1.1).

Japan earned the United Nations' (UN) description of an *ageing society* in 1970. The UN defines an *ageing society* as a society with people 65 years and older comprising over 7% of its total population. By 1995, Japan's societal ageing had reached 14.5%, exceeding the UN's definition of an *aged society* of 14% (Management and Coordination Agency, 1995). The speed of Japan's societal ageing has been phenomenal. It has taken only 25 years for Japan to double its ageing rates from 7 to

14.5% (between 1970 and 1995), compared with 115 years for France and 66 years for the United States. Japan will continue to age rapidly over the next 30 years, and at a greater rate than many other developed societies (US Bureau of the Census, 1993) (Figure 1.1).

Table 1.1 Percentage of the older population (65 and over) in the total population (forecast for 2010 and 2025)

	1970	1990	2010	2025
Japan	7.1	11.8	21.3	26.7
Sweden	13.7	18.0	19.6	23.7
France	12.9	14.6	17.2	22.6
Singapore	3.4	5.8	10.4	20.6
United States	9.8	12.5	13.3	18.7
Rep. of Korea	3.3	4.8	9.0	15.2
China	4.3	5.8	8.3	13.3
India	3.7	3.7	5.3	7.8
Kenya	3.9	2.2	2.7	3.8

Source: US Bureau of the Census. (1993), *An Aging World II*.

Figure 1.1 International comparison of ageing rates of society (%)

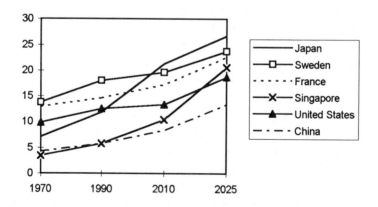

Source: US Bureau of the Census. (1993), *An Aging World II*.

In addition to changes in the age structure of the population, Japan's post-war economic growth brought rapid industrialization and urbanization, and with it associated changes in social values and lifestyles. One significant issue is the transformation of living arrangements. The vast majority of people in Japan used to spend their later life living with their children, and approximately 60% of older people still live intergenerationally. The socio-economic changes, however, have broken down the traditional family structure, and the number of elderly-only households[3] has increased rapidly. If the traditional arrangement of coresidency is no longer the only housing option for Japanese people in later life, what is required to accommodate such a transition?

The disproportional growth of the older population and its accompanying changes in lifestyles pose a considerable challenge to the nation's housing, employment, and welfare policies since existing socio-economic and legal systems have become obsolete and can no longer meet the people's ever-changing immediate and long-term needs (Ageing Sogo Kenkyu Centre, 1995; Coleman and Salt, 1992). Furthermore, as the ageing of the population advances, the economy may suffer supply-side economic problems caused by an increased social security burden, a shortage of savings, and both a decline and ageing of the working population[4] (Maruo, 1992). Issues of an ageing society have become primary concerns for Japanese society ahead of the twenty-first century.

Older people in the 1990s have witnessed major changes in Japanese society – from the devastation and defeat of the Second World War to the birth of the world's second economic superpower. The economic growth brought affluence to the nation, and the ranks of 'middle-class' people in Japan swelled. According to the OECD's *Economic Outlook, Occasional Studies* (1976), by the late 1960s, Japan had already achieved a Gini coefficient of 0.316 (after taxes),[5] to rank as one of the leading nations in the world with respect to egalitarian distribution of income (Nakagawa, 1979). Although the development of post-war housing, employment, and welfare policies successfully raised the living standards of Japanese people, those policies also helped to create new forms of social stratification and reinforced gender roles. Gender inequality in the family and society has remained a significant feature of Japanese society, with women's dependency on their working husbands continuing throughout the process of post-war industrialization.

Japan's economic miracle has been achieved largely at the sacrifice of the family. The male breadwinner family model developed to maximize family resources. The government also promoted this model in order to achieve full employment rates by excluding women from the labour market. It was believed that gender roles among married couples helped to sustain an efficient and strong male labour force. In fact, without the domestic support of their wives, few *kigyou-senshi* [corporate warriors],[6] who dedicated themselves to their company, often working for long hours, and sometimes until their death from work-related stress or fatigue, would not have been able to participate fully in Japan's post-war economic miracle.

Family resources have continued to substitute for an under-developed welfare system in post-war Japan. This was largely due to Japan's traditional pattern of coresidency between adult children and older parents, which provided a perfect arena for family support. Again, the emphasis of gender roles made this arrangement possible, since family tradition used to define a woman's role as that of welfare provider. In modern society, however, socio-economic changes, such as increasing labour force participation by women, are eroding the efficacy of the Japanese family, and transforming family relations. Gender inequality among married couples remains a contentious issue for women of recent generations. As a result of women's increasing financial independence, marriage rates of younger women have started declining sharply over the last decade. Half of women in their late 20s were single in 1995, an increase from 30% in 1985 (Management and Coordination Agency, 1985; 1995).

This book explores the transformation of family relations from the traditional family system to the modern family patterns of the 1990s in the context of post-war socio-economic and demographic changes. With the recent decline of marriage rates and the breakdown of traditional coresidency, it is evident that these transformations have been occurring not only in people's norms and values but also in actual practice. Family relations are further analysed in the context of post-war welfare state development. In sustaining the family as a welfare resource, the Japanese welfare state has developed in distinct ways when compared with other industrial societies. The importance of institutional forces in reshaping the family and society is examined, since these issues are linked to the welfare circumstances of women of the pre-war generation, particularly those who are currently disadvantaged. Finally, new demographic trends and changing family traditions are analysed in relation to housing choices and constraints for older people. Post-war housing policies have emphasized the promotion of home ownership, and constrained people's residential choices. The underdeveloped welfare state also played its part in perpetuating the traditional form of coresidency. Since post-war socio-economic changes inevitably shifted away from coresidency, there has been an increasing need to seek housing alternatives for people in later life.

The material contained in this book was collected using both primary and secondary research methods, with a bilingual approach of English and Japanese. The above issues were explored through a series of in-depth interviews with older women. Considering that this particular cohort of women had lived through both the inter-war and post-war periods, recording their experiences of social change in their own words was particularly interesting and needed to be conducted before this generation is replaced with post-war generations. The informants were selected from three different welfare sectors (the family, the market and the state) in order to make a clear distinction among older women in terms of their socio-economic status, tenure and dwelling type, family relations and living arrangements. Further interviews were carried out with middle-aged women, policy makers, policy implementors and service providers for older people to supplement the interviews conducted with the older women. Further details on methodology and approach are provided in Appendix A.

The fieldwork was conducted in Kitakyushu, Japan for five months over 1996 and 1997. It is located at the north-eastern end of Kyushu, and the population is approximately one million people in an area of 482 km^2. An urban location was chosen because older people in such areas have been more affected by recent social, economic, and political changes in modern society. Since regional, or urban-rural differences tend to exist in Japanese people's values and lifestyles as well as in the policy implementation process, it must be acknowledged that the findings of the case study, however, may not have been representative of older Japanese people as a whole.

Kitakyushu, one of the 13 largest cities (Table 1.2) designated by the national government, was founded in 1963 with the amalgamation of five cities. It was initially the largest city in Kyushu. It is an industrial and trading city with rich natural resources. The city's industrial sector originally developed on the basis of heavy and large-scale industry with the opening of the nationally-owned Yawata Iron Works in 1897. In more modern times, however, the city has not kept up with the nationwide structural changes that have taken place in industry, and thus the city's urban growth has lagged behind. This is illustrated by the decreasing population trend of the city (Figure 1.2). Since 1988 revitalization programs have been introduced to attract investment and population into the city in response to the declining population. The emphasis of such plans included the promotion of higher quality or more fine industries in addition to existing industries through public-private partnership, the support of medium and small enterprises financially, and the promotion of tourism and convention (conference) industries.

Table 1.2 Population of the 13 designated cities in Japan in 1995

Japan	125,570,246	Kobe	1,423,792
Tokyo	7,967,614	Fukuoka	1,284,795
Yokohama	3,307,136	Kawasaki	1,202,820
Osaka	2,602,421	Hiroshima	1,108,888
Nagoya	2,152,186	Kitakyushu	1,019,598
Sapporo	1,757,025	Sendai	971,297
Kyoto	1,463,822	Chiba	856,878

Source: Management and Coordination Agency, Japan. (1995), *Kokusei Chousa [Population Census of Japan]*.

Figure 1.2 Population decrease of Kitakyushu (1970-95)

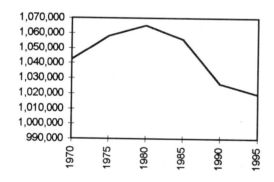

Sources: Management and Coordination Agency, Japan. (1985, 1990, 1995), *Kokusei Chousa [Population Census of Japan]*; Office of the Prime Minister, Japan. (1970, 1975, 1980), *Kokusei Chousa [Population Census of Japan]*.

There were two main reasons why Kitakyushu was chosen to be the fieldwork location. First, the city's demographic trends matched the national trends more closely than other cities. Migration out-flows were, however, higher on average than in-flows to the city. Due to the decline of the city's major industry, a considerable proportion of the younger working population left the city. Along with other factors such as increased longevity and decreasing birth-rates, the population of the city was, therefore, rapidly ageing. The speed of ageing in the city had been faster than that of the national average and other designated cities (Figure 1.3). In 1995, the city's annual rate of societal ageing was 15.7% (Table 1.3), and the rate was projected to increase to 20% within 10 years (City of Kitakyushu, 1994).

Figure 1.3   Comparative rates of older population in 12 designated cities in 1995 (%)

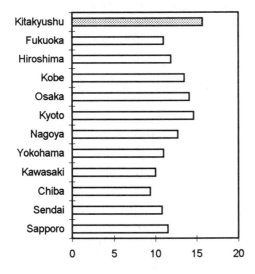

Source: Management and Coordination Agency, Japan. (1995), *Kokusei Chousa [Population Census of Japan]*.

A transformation had also been occurring in the lifestyles of older people in Kitakyushu. Consequently, elderly-only households had been growing rapidly in both number and proportion of total households, as had the national trends (Figure 1.4). However, both the growth rate and proportion were again higher in the city (56% of total households) than the national average (41%) (Management and Coordination Agency, 1995). Therefore, both existing and potential problems surrounding the issues of an 'aged society' in Japan were likely to be highlighted and addressed in the case of Kitakyushu, having entered an 'aged society' state earlier.

Table 1.3 Percentages of older population (65 years and over) in Kitakyushu (1970-95)

	1970	1980	1990	1995
Total Population	1,042,321	1,065,078	1,026,455	1,019,598
Population over 65	61,703	92,691	130,423	160,584
Ageing Rates (%)	5.9	8.7	12.7	15.7

Sources: Management and Coordination Agency, Japan. (1985, 1990, 1995), *Kokusei Chousa [Population Census of Japan]*; Office of the Prime Minister, Japan. (1970, 1975, 1980), *Kokusei Chousa [Population Census of Japan]*.

Figure 1.4 Percentage of elderly-only households in Kitakyushu

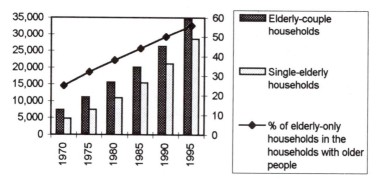

Note: Older people who are living with other older people (relatives or friends) but not as couples, or who are living in institutional facilities or hospitals are excluded.

Source: Management and Coordination Agency, Japan. (1970, 1975, 1980, 1985, 1990, 1995), *Kokusei Chousa [Population Census of Japan]*.

The second main reason why Kitakyushu was chosen was a rapid change in the implementation structure of national policy by local authorities. The above transformations had made the city officials aware of the problems caused by the new trends, and they began to propose positive policy responses. Since the late 1980s, Kitakyushu had been developing policies for older people in accordance with the national 10-year Gold Plan (see Chapter 6). Recent initiatives to promote independent living for older people included the provision of *Itawari Juutaku* (Silver Housing); special loans and mortgage programs to encourage traditional extended family living arrangements; housing adaptation programs to enable older people to remain in their own dwellings; an improved community care scheme (e.g. the 24 hour home help dispatch service); and the establishment of a Health and Welfare Centre with an 'advisory corner for older people' in each ward office. The city was, therefore, able to provide good samples of older people who had benefited from those new and progressive policy responses. On the other hand, the research in the city did not exclude other older people to whom the new initiatives were not effective. In light of the limited public resources, there were also older people who had to cope with ordinary or poorly-equipped housing without any particular support.

The book presents three key themes – *changing family tradition, the development of the welfare state, and housing choices and constraints for older people* – in chapters two, four, and six, respectively. Each of these three chapters is linked to an empirical chapter three, five, and seven, respectively, using material from in-depth interviews. The final chapter concludes with a discussion of conceptual and policy issues.

In this book, Japanese names appear in their Japanese order (family name first) except when citing publications in English, in which case the author's name appears in Western order. In chapters three, five, and seven, where empirical evidence is presented, individual informants are referred to by their initials and ages in quotations. Web-site references are cited with their address (URL) and the date of access. All Japanese words are italicised in the text (with translations when first used) and do not take definite or indefinite articles. A complete glossary also appears in Appendix B.

Notes

1   Older people are defined in this book as anyone 65 years and older. Japanese people traditionally defined old age as being 60 years and older, as did most of the other societies influenced by Chinese culture (Maeda, 1993). The sixty-first year after birth, called *kanreki* [return of the calendar], was often regarded as the beginning of a person's second childhood. Nowadays, in Japan, as in most developed societies,

people usually take their first or final retirement and become dependent on a pension at the age of 60 to 65. Japanese researchers also tend to use the age of 65 as a dividing line between middle age and old age.

2   The population replacement rate (the number of children necessary to maintain the same population size) is 2.1 live births per woman. In Japan, it went below this number in the early 1970s (http://www.jinjapan.org/insight/html/, 1 October 1997).

3   Elderly-only households are ones which consist of only those 65 years and older (whether couples or one-person members) with or without other unmarried family member(s) under 18 years of age.

4   The burden of dependency in a population is defined as the ratio of the number of dependent children (15 and below) and retired persons (65 and over) to the numbers in 'productive' age groups. Since the productive age groups include full-time students and housewives, but do not count older people still engaged in paid work, the ratio can be misleading.

5   This same survey showed Sweden at 0.302 (1972), France at 0.414 (1970), and America at 0.381 (1972).

6   A metaphor used pejoratively to describe the characteristics of Japanese salaried workers. On average, Japanese people work 1,966 hours a year, about 370 hours more than Germans (http://www.mofa.go.jp/socsec/ogawa.html, 8 December 1997).

2 Social Change and Family Change

Introduction

Each society has a distinct process of development. Post-war Japan has been, in many ways, one of the fastest moving societies in the world. The development of Japanese society is unique among other industrial nations in that it progressed from an agricultural society to a technologically-advanced industrial one in a relatively short period of time. From 1955 to the first oil crisis in 1973, the Japanese economy enjoyed an average annual growth of 10%, a rate unparalleled in the Western world (Berggren and Nomura, 1997). The national goal in the 1960s was explicitly high-speed economic growth with the slogan, '*oubei ni, oitsuke, oikose*' [catch up and overtake Europe and America].

Despite the recession in the early 1970s, the Japanese economy recovered quickly and entered a second period of prosperity in the 1980s with successful industrial restructuring. In the second half of the 1980s, Japan enjoyed a new period of high economic growth, peaking at 5.6% in the fiscal year 1990 – this period is known as the 'bubble-economy'.[1] Since the steep decline in the stock market, and the bursting of the speculative real estate bubble in the early 1990s, Japan has been suffering its most serious recession since the Second World War (http://www.jinjapan.org/insight/html/, 28 May 1998). For the first time since 1974, Japan's economy shrank by 0.7% during the fiscal year 1997 (*BBC News*, 12 June 1998).

Certainly, the remarkable speed of post-war industrialization helped to shape the fundamental character of modern Japanese society. In an agricultural society, geographic and social mobility are relatively minimal until modernization brings social changes (Giele, 1982; Lawton et al, 1994; Sussman et al, 1980). In Japan, before post-war industrialization, the majority of families were of the extended type, and society was relatively

11

static. Family structure and relationships within the family have not, however, remained static in the post-war period. Japan's vigorous post-war economic growth brought rapid industrialization and then urbanization. Sometimes referred to as the 'Westernization' of life, this transformation deeply affected the social and economic lives of people of all classes, in both rural and urban communities (Maeda, 1993). As nations become more modernized, the dominant family structure subsequently decreases in size. One of the results is an expansion of nuclear family households.

In Japan, many traditional features of society still remain prominent in areas such as family businesses, occupational welfare, family and community-based support. The development of post-war society has created a unique coalescence of westernized lifestyles bounded by traditional social and family values.

Modernization and Social Change

Modernization theory as applied to ageing issues indicates that there are systematic relations between the extent of modernization of a society and the status and condition of older people (Cowgill, 1974; 1986; Cowgill and Holmes, 1972). The following factors are usually regarded as having influenced the fundamental nature of Japanese society over the last century.

Industrial Restructuring

Post-war industrial restructuring brought significant social change, particularly influencing the employment pattern and employment system of Japanese workers. Under the pre-war economic conditions, especially in rural areas, the family formation was an extended type and industry was predominantly primary such as farming and household industries.

The changing social and economic pressures experienced by industrialized nations throughout the world has also taken its toll on Japan. The Japanese economy has made great progress since 1955, only 10 years after the end of the Second World War and Japan's widespread industrial destruction. Between 1955 and 1970, Japan's industrial production expanded 6.7 times (Oouchi et al, 1971). Even after the first oil crisis of 1973, the Japanese economy continued to develop rapidly until the recent 'post-bubble' recession in the early 1990s. With post-war industrialization, significant change has occurred in the composition of industry in which the working population[2] engaged. Workers in primary industries declined from 49% in 1950 to 11% in 1980. Instead, the proportions employed in secondary industries rose from 22% to 34%; and those in tertiary industries from 30% to 55% over the same period (Kendig, 1989) (Figure 2.1). Furthermore, the number of workers who were self-employed or in family industries declined from 59% in 1950 to 29% in 1980. Currently, approximately 90% of the working population in Japan are employees.

Figure 2.1 Changing proportions of workers engaged in different sectors (%)

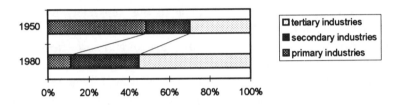

Source: Kendig. (1989), *Social Change and Family Dependency in Old Age*, p. 8

Industrial restructuring brought change to the socio-economic structure of Japanese society (Maeda and Shimizu, 1992). The transformation affected the position and status of older people in the family and society. In agricultural societies, the economic value of knowledge and experience relative to physical prowess was generally high. Collective production and collective consumption were also the norm. Labour force participation rates for older people were, therefore, generally high, which represented their relatively strong economic position in the family and society (Ogawa, 1992). Moving away from an agricultural society, families began to lose control over material resources such as land and agricultural production, which traditionally used to employ, support, and sustain older people in the family (Giele, 1982). Industrialization has resulted in the predominance of a cash economy with an employed working system, which has led to improved living standards. The introduction of a compulsory retirement system has excluded older people from the economic benefits and other privileges of employment. Consequently, reduced or fixed incomes, combined with other age-related losses and risks such as illness and widowhood, have placed older people in a position of multiple disadvantage (Hashimoto and Kendig,

1992). Moreover, in a modern industrial society where the majority of the workforce is engaged in second or tertiary industries, the older and younger generations usually have separate incomes, and different lifestyles resulting from different occupations. The improved living standards produced by a cash economy have also lessened the status of older people, who used to represent the family lineage and a traditional tie to the land (Kamo, 1988).

The traditional extended family has weakened in its structure. Some scholars have explained the reason behind decreasing rates of extended family living mainly as the result of the transformation of the socio-economic structure, or as an expansion of numbers of newly married couples, rather than the transformation of family ideology (Harada, 1987; Okamoto et al, 1993). As a result of industrial restructuring, it has become natural and convenient for both generations to live separately under the above economic circumstances (Kamada and Sasaki, 1990; Nakane, 1972). The extended family living arrangement was practical and cost-effective for the pre-war family members who shared the same occupations in primary (or household) industries. The purpose and importance behind living with other generations has, however, been diminishing due partly to the expansion of the salaried working population. Many contemporary families with their own businesses, however, still retain such traditions (Suzuki, 1989).

Technological Development

It has been argued that the status and support of older people are undermined by social change introduced by *new technologies* (Cowgill and Holmes, 1972). The power and authority of older people are said to be eroded as new cohorts entering adulthood control emergent forms of knowledge and economic production. The accumulation of experience and wisdom is most valuable in a more stable society. When technology changes rapidly, experience becomes less important. Younger people are therefore less disadvantaged to compete with their seniors in both their workplace and their living situations.

Advancements in technology have introduced many labour-saving appliances into households which have improved people's quality of life and living standards. Such appliances require less time to be set aside for daily domestic work than in the past. This reduces the burden of work on unpaid domestic workers, usually female members of the family, and encourages them to take up paid work outside the home. Additionally, one of the advantages of coresidency was offering a means of providing mutual support for generations in the household. As domestic work has become less demanding, this has reduced the usefulness of older people in an extended family household. Estimates show that even in the early period of industrialization 20% of older people were not involved in day-to-day family routines or interacted in extended family living (Plath, 1972).

Urban-Rural Mobility

In many societies, urbanization and economic development caused a rise in urban-rural mobility and facilitated occupational mobility (Davis and van den Oever, 1981). In the process of industrialization, the family became more differentiated from the extension of the market system and economic production. This increased the exit of younger people from rural areas to the major cities for purposes of higher education and employment, and the development of much greater mobility than was previously known in the traditional agricultural societies. The proportion of the Japanese population in urban areas rose rapidly from 37% in 1950 to 76% in 1980 (Ogawa, 1986). Once people gain employment in urban areas, they tend to stay in those areas. Today, nearly 80% of Japan's 125 million people live in cities (and their suburbs) throughout the country (http://www.jinjapan.org/insight/html/, 28 May 1998). In recent years, however, some medium-size cities have tried to increase return-migration levels by organizing recruitment fairs and offering career counselling.

Urban-rural mobility creates geographic distances between the generations which again breakdown traditional living arrangements, weaken intergenerational relations, and possibly lessen the moral pressures applying in traditional society (Davis and van den Oever, 1981; Kendig, 1989; Ogawa, 1992). Occupational mobility is also likely to place parents and offspring in different occupations, resulting in different social classes.

Labour Force Participation

The increasing labour force participation of women is another outcome of industrialization, and has contributed to the transformation of the family formation and function. The post-war period has seen a major shift in female employment away from farming and unpaid domestic work to paid work outside the home. The number of women holding a paid job outside of farming grew by 74% between 1960 and 1975 (Holden, 1983). In 1991, the labour force participation by women aged between 15 and 64 years reached over 50% (Sugimoto, 1997). As a result, many women are no longer just entitled to welfare benefits by virtue of their dependent status within the family as wives and mothers. Nowadays, married women, especially middle-aged women over 35 years old, are likely to take up paid work after child-rearing, and their financial contribution to the household has changed their position in the family and their relation with their husband (for further reference, see Chapter 4).

Women who have entered the labour force at a rapid rate in the last couple of decades are often the principal care providers for older parents (Economic Planning Agency, 1982). Due to the implicit public emphasis on traditional family values as a welfare provider, social services for child care and old-age care have been much less developed than those in Western countries (Maeda, 1993). Traditionally, therefore, career women have faced the heavy burdens of both family obligations and paid work. Their willingness or feeling of *giri* [obligations] to care for their older parents often jeopardized or restricted their labour force participation or career development.

Demographic Change

A rapid demographic transition is another post-war phenomenon impacting on the Japanese family and society. Longevity is directly and significantly linked to modernization: rising incomes, advanced medicine, and improved sanitation and nutrition brought better health and prolonged average life expectancy. In Japan, the birth-rate has also decreased very sharply since 1950, due to increased female labour participation, higher standards of living and education costs, and changing lifestyles. The low birth-rate, combined with increased life expectancy, has brought about a sharp increase in the proportion of the older population. Consequently, ageing has become a prime policy agenda in Japanese society in the 1990s. As Shouji (1993) quoted:

> ...(s)ocietal ageing had not been an issue until 1959. The term of '*roujin mondai*' [an issue for older people] had not even existed in Japanese policy debate until the 1960s.   (Shouji, 1993, p. 191)

For society as a whole, modernization has degraded the status of older people by loosening the taut equilibrium that existed in primitive societies between the length of useful life-span and the capacity of society to sustain it (Giele, 1982). In post-war society, a combination of factors (e.g.

modernization of the family, increased longevity, and underdeveloped social services) has placed much heavier demands by older people on existing family resources, especially in the area of old-age care.

Value Shift

Social change brought by modernization has promoted a shift to individualistic values along the lines of western societies, which has reduced the security and status of older people (Cowgill, 1986; Cowgill and Holmes, 1972; Giele, 1982). Although some Japanese individuals moved away from traditional values as they grew older in modern society, the major source of shifting values appeared to be the succession of new cohorts having more modern views.

Educational practice played a part in reinforcing traditional family beliefs and 'selflessness' in Japan (Lebra and Sugiyama, 1979). In contrast to the pre-war Confucian education (e.g. filial piety, respect for seniority) at school and in the family, post-war education placed more emphasis on modern values, such as being "independent, without relying on other people" (Kamada and Sasaki, 1990). In addition, the new education system shifted the emphasis from households to schools. Such a system and its associated ideology resulted in parents holding less authority and influence over their children compared with parents in the past. It has further reduced the usefulness of older people, since children may have turned more to schools than older people for knowledge and values appropriate to the new economic era (Kendig, 1989; Sano, 1958).

Therefore, the modern views of the younger generations have tended to widen the generation gap that existed over many customs and beliefs. Structural change of the family (from extended family living to the nuclear family) also leads to behavioural change which in turn reshapes expectations in family relations, including family support (Kendig, 1989). Having little in common with the more individualistic and 'Westernized' younger Japanese, true communication between generations becomes very difficult (Reischauer, 1977).

Definition of the Family

A definition of a family formation is rather complex in any society. The nuclear family can be defined as a single set of parents and their immediate offspring. It is the most common family formation found in highly industrial societies. The nuclear family is an independent operating social unit which is often residentially and socially separated from other family units and parental families (Das and Bardis, 1978). The conventional form of extended family, on the other hand, includes three or more generations of family members living together under the same roof: typically, grandparents, parent, and children. The structural and functional characteristics of the family are, however, often more complex. In some societies such as those of a Hispanic or Indian origin, the extended family is identified more in terms of its structure, including 'joint families' with two kin-related nuclear families of a horizontal relationship living in the same house (Garcia, 1993). In Japan, even coresidency between older parents and their younger family members is no longer the only convention. Today, many of the arrangements are neither 'intergenerational' nor 'extended,' since contemporary situations include older parents living with their unmarried adult children.

In post-war Japan, family formation has become more dynamic than in the pre-war periods. It is, in part, explained by the higher geographic mobility of younger generations (for educational and occupational purposes) and people's greater adaptability to changes in their personal circumstances (e.g. widowhood and ill-health). Some families, therefore, transform their household structure over time according to their needs. For example, older parents may start living with their adult children when they need family support in old age. Despite increased preferences for independence, older people may only be temporarily separated from their younger families and, indeed, may be at risk of becoming dependents in their old age (Hashimoto, 1993; Masuda, 1979). Also, a company-related transfer may divide a nuclear family temporarily since *tanshin-funin* [proceeding to one's new post without one's family] is relatively common in Japan.

The ambiguity inherent in the structural concept of the extended family is further complicated when functional criteria are added. Although the extended family is structurally defined as above, the weakened functional aspects of family relations discount the definition of the extended family. Functional criteria vary depending on whether families exchange resources or if they simply interact on a regular basis, regardless of physical closeness (Garcia, 1993). In recent years, even within coresident households, two generations often have more individual space, and more separate lifestyles and finances than previous generations in coresident situations (see Chapter 6). Indeed, the term 'coresidency'[3] used throughout the book does not exclude various other forms of 'modified extended families'.

Historical Perspective: Feudalism and Confucianism

In Japan, the basis of the traditional family system was laid down mirroring the social structure and hierarchy of the day. In the *Edo* period[4] (1603-1867), Japanese society was familistic and predominantly feudal, and even the family was also feudal in its structure. In fact, this familistic structure and the patriarchal stem family system were based on Confucian doctrines, and especially reinforced by the warrior and upper classes (Maykovich, 1978). This structure and system have had a lasting impact on the Japanese family throughout the twentieth century.

The feudal social system was characterized as follows (Goode, 1963). First, its social ranks were closed and people remained in the position into which they were born. Second, there was a hierarchy of positions of power, so that from the lowest to the highest there was an unbroken chain of obedience upwards and protection downwards. Third, goods and services, including the ownership of land, were distributed on the basis of the social ranks to be found within this hierarchy of power and responsibility. Also, the basic rules applied to the family as the last link in the chain of hierarchy. This system restricted individual or family wishes and decisions not to conflict with those of the state and society.

During the *Meiji* Restoration, which commenced in 1868, political power moved from feudal lords to the Emperor government. The *Meiji* government realized the necessity of catching up with Western culture, and of becoming economically competitive with the Western world (Maykovich, 1978). Hence, the government encouraged Western ideas, and supported industrialization. In 1889, the Constitution was promulgated, and a new Civil code adopted in 1898. The Civil code continued to emphasize Confucian ideals and helped the spread of familistic nationalism based on worship of the Emperor as a living deity. Consequently, the idea of the stem family was imposed not only on the warrior and upper classes, but also over all the social classes (Koyama, 1962; Ohashi and Masuda, 1968).

Confucianism was certainly one of the key features reinforcing Japanese society and the family throughout the *Meiji* period (1868-1912). The Japanese viewed it more from an ethical perspective than a religious one, and held virtues such as loyalty to the state or the Emperor, filial piety, faith in friendship and family, and respect for seniority, as most important (Morishima, 1988). For example, the Confucian ideology of the obedience of children to their parents and parents-in-law was regarded as an expression of *oya-koukou* [filial piety] (Sussman et al, 1980). It was an extremely important moral virtue corresponding to the infinite grace of parents including the grace of bearing, nurturing, and allowing marriage. Filial piety also applied to the moral aspect of coresidency.

Moreover, Confucianism requires harmony primarily concerning the individual's relationship to various groups and communities, and denies individualism. Therefore, people must hold back their individual needs and desires, in order to emphasize the positive aspects of groups and organizations, and to maximize their benefits. The ability of the Japanese to assimilate Western technology and science with astonishing speed after the *Meiji* Restoration was due, in part, to such Confucian orientation (Borthwick, 1992; Morishima, 1988). Perhaps Japan was one of few nations which had been able to use its family value system positively in the process of industrialization (Goode, 1963; Levy, 1955; Rozman, 1992). For example, the notion of 'firm-as-family' was developed and consistent with one of the central political concepts of the *Meiji* period. The system expanded in the post-war periods, reinforced by the development of *shuushin-koyou* [life-time employment system] and *nenkou-joretsu* [seniority system in promotion and income] in the workplace. This analogy of 'firm-as-family' has, however, become less significant since the Japanese family itself has changed and no longer exerts the same hold over people's day-to-day lives (Clark, 1979).

Family disorganization was not, therefore, serious or widespread during the early period of post-war industrialization. At the time, traditional family values were unchanged compared to the significant changes that had occurred in the material aspects of Japanese culture. However, gradually but noticeably, such Confucian values started to be transformed as industrialization and Westernization advanced.

The Japanese Family System: *Ie*

In Japan, the *Ie* system was a traditional concept of the family system, backed by the Confucian idea of gratitude (Nakane, 1972; Nasu and Yazawa, 1973). The Japanese word *Ie* has several meanings including family, household, lineage, home and house. In referring to the *Ie* ideology in this book, however, the word exclusively means lineage, which is conceptualized as continuously succeeding from generation to generation (Koyano, 1996). Many aspects of this system made it unique from other family systems.

Family Continuity

Until the *Meiji* Civil code, the *Ie* system was an authority structure in which the paternal head of household held authority, with a rule of one-son succession (Nakane, 1974). An extended family living with the successor family, frequently the eldest son's family, was the usual form of living arrangement. Typically, older parents lived with their eldest son, his wife and children, and sometimes included their unmarried (or divorced) adult children. Indeed, a dominant value in traditional society was the biological perpetuation of the patrilineal system (Maykovich, 1978).

It was the duty of the eldest son, as the designated successor to the household, to perpetuate the family collectively, as family name, assets, social status of the family, and occupation were usually inherited by him. Thus, the greatest part of the family property and wealth were passed on, undivided, to the eldest son and his immediate family. The *Ie* system of passing the family holding down intact provided for family continuity without impoverishing *Ie* by constant subdivisions. Responsibility for *haka* [the tomb] and *butsudan* [a Buddhist altar in the home in which mortuary tables of ancestors were placed] was also taken by the eldest son in order to continue the ancestor worship of lineage. Because family continuity was important, families with no children adopted a child, and those families who had no son adopted *youshi* [son-in-law] not only to marry their daughter, but also to take their surname, and finally to succeed as household head. Because of the one-son succession rule, a household including more than one married couple of the same generation such as married brothers or sisters was uncommon in Japan (Nakane, 1972). Surprisingly, this system still survives in some families of rural communities in modern Japan.

Ie prescribed family domination and individual submission in the selection of marriage partners, the behaviour of wives, and the dissolution of marriages. Under the *Ie* system, the purpose of marriage was predominantly one of family continuity, and the position and role of family members were fixed around the benefits it brought. Individual wishes and choices were ignored for the interest and the benefit of the family (Maykovich, 1978; Nakane, 1974). A bride, especially the bride of the first son, was commonly referred to as *'uchi no yome'* [our *Ie*'s bride] for she was not only the bride of her husband, but the bride of the entire family (Vogel, 1965). Thus, instead of creating a new family, the bride (of the eldest son) usually moved into her husband's *Ie*. In order to retain the tradition, therefore, arranged marriage was the predominant way of acquiring a partner in the pre-war society. To find suitable partners for their children, families usually relied on a matchmaker, and weighed up criteria such as compatibility in terms of wealth and social status of the two families, the occupation and income of a young man, or the health and appearance of the girl. From such a perspective, marriage and parenthood in Japan were not in the least love relationships, but partnerships directed to serve the family's goals and needs (Hareven, 1982).

In terms of divorce, the previous high divorce rate of pre-war Japan was related to the pattern of *Ie* sending back the bride if she was not satisfactory or incompatible with the family (Vogel, 1965). In particular, failure to bear an heir had a catastrophic impact upon the outcome of a marriage under such a traditional family system. In case of divorce, the bride's original *Ie* became responsible for her welfare once again. Japan is, therefore, one of the few nations where the divorce rate had gone down in the democratization process and with the abolition of the *Ie* system. In the 1960s, about one in ten marriages ended in divorce, which was approximately one-third the rate of 1885 (Vogel, 1965).

Marriage was a contractual rather than a spiritual or emotional attachment between a husband and a wife. Its importance lay in reinforcing the traditional family system with strong normative values of pre-war Japan. Expecting little emotional satisfaction from marriage, except traditional family duties and responsibilities, Japanese couples were likely to achieve contentment (Goode, 1963).

Inequality among Family Members

Traditionally, the *Ie* system was formed to maximize the use of available family resources, and it was especially well adapted to rural land conditions (Vogel, 1965). This self-help approach by the family was crucial at times in order to sustain themselves without alternative support. The family was responsible for the economic support as well as the welfare of all its members, and duties included care for family members in case of illness or unemployment. Under the circumstances, inequality among family members depending on their gender and seniority was inevitable.

Typically, the older father was the household head with the legal power to rule over other family members. The position, power, and privileges of the household head also provided the means to fulfill his obligations of maintaining the family name, assets, and social status in order to pass them over to the next generation (Koyano, 1996). Among children, especially those of farmers, there was also a strict dividing line between successor and non-successor members. The eldest son was given a superior position as the future head of the household. Compared to non-successor siblings, the eldest son was usually brought up with extra care and privileges as well as onerous duties and obligations. In addition, before urbanization, members in a large household other than successors were simply accommodated in the house as labourers, rather than as family members of equal status (Nakane, 1972). With the expansion of industrial establishments in urban areas, non-successor members usually became wage earners and migrated out to urban areas, changing the family structure in rural society.

Equality in terms of status and role was also applied to women within households. Their status varied according to age and marital status. Daughters did not have the same status as sons in the family since they were considered to be temporary family members (or properties) until their marriage. Even after marriage, women did not have an equal right of decision-making in the household because of the male-dominated nature of family tradition. A position of a new bride in the family was very low to start with, and tremendous effort had to be made by her to adapt to her new *Ie*'s *kafuu* [family rules and customs]. A wife of the household head was required to serve and be obedient to her parents-in-law, and her husband as the household heir (Koyano, 1996). Despite the norms, blood relations were often stronger than marriage bond. For example, even unmarried or divorced daughters in their original family were in a more privileged position than a new bride. Once her husband succeeded the household and became the head of the household, the bride acquired considerable power, especially over the areas of household management and finance. Historically, lower class women used to be less subordinate than those in upper classes.

The Contemporary Family in Transition

Abolition of the Ie System

Although the traditional family elements remained deeply embedded in the social structure of the Japanese, post-war socio-economic and legal changes inevitably brought new ideology, functions, and relations into the family. A fundamental change in family values occurred after the defeat in the Second World War and the following US occupation (Maykovich, 1978). US influence was remarkable in democratizing traditional Japanese society. As a part of the process, the *Ie* ideology was officially renounced, and the concept of *Ie* was completely removed from the new Constitution in 1946, the new Civil code in 1947, and the Family and Inheritance Law in 1948.

Instead, the revised law stressed the importance of individual rights and equality among family members at the expense of the family collectivity. For example, the new Constitution declares that agreement between the couple is the only basis of marriage, and the legal responsibilities of the marriage are set out to protect a spouse (in most cases, the wife) and children rather than the older parents of a husband. After *Ie* was abolished, the traditional system of adopting *youshi* husbands also became invalid at the same time. Thus, the definition of the family shifted legally from the extended family of the paternal lineage to a nuclear family under the new Civil code. Even though adult children still have a legal responsibility to their older parents in terms of need, it is of lesser importance than responsibility to their spouse and children.

This new system was encouraged by a different economic pattern of family life where the succession of the household had little functional meaning, especially in urban areas (Nakane, 1972). Also, the institution of a democratic education system probably added to the transformations occurring in family life (Maykovich, 1978). In general, these legal changes led the Japanese family away from a traditional system symbolized by the Emperor, to a more egalitarian and individualistic one exibiting greater equality, for example, when dealing with matters of inheritance for children. It also liberated family members from the totalitarian authority of the family (Matsumoto, 1968; Maykovich, 1978; Sano, 1958).

Family Democracy

With the abolition of the *Ie* system, individual choices and wishes have been expanded in many aspects of the lives of the Japanese people in post-war society. Parental authority ceased to dominate or became less influential over children's decisions. Marriage is one significant example where transformation has occurred. Partner selection has become more of an individual choice than family benefits or continuity, even though many young people still consult with their parents and make the decision jointly. Although traditional arranged marriages still remain in modern society, the arrangements have become less formal and the individual voice of young people is heard more often and is more widely respected. Today, less than 30% of the marriages are arranged marriages (Figure 2.2).

Second, post-war divorce is increasingly becoming a mutual matter between a couple rather than a family decision. According to the new Civil code, women have equal rights concerning divorce and there are increasing cases in which wives initiate divorce. The divorce rate has progressively increased since the 1960s, reaching a post-war peak in the early 1980s (Sugimoto, 1997). Perhaps, it has become a more socially acceptable option, with less stigma attached to divorcees than previously was the case.

Figure 2.2 A change in the ratio of arranged marriages and marriages for love (1949-83) (%)

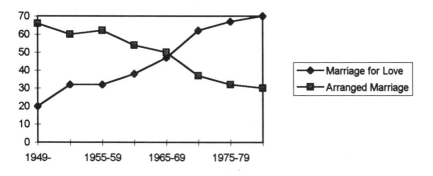

Source: Yazawa. "Family Issues in Modern-day Japan with Figures." (http://www.jinjapan.org/insight/html/, 28 May 1998)

As women gain economic independence through their participation in the labour force, they are more likely to divorce when marriage is not working out satisfactorily. For those women, the social costs of divorce are calculated to be less than the benefits which divorce may bring. As a result of the democratization of family patterns and ideology, the number of divorces based on incompatibility between the married couple or infidelity has increased (Maykovich, 1978; Ohashi and Masuda, 1968).

Compared with other industrial societies, however, the divorce rate still remains very low (Table 2.1). Such a low divorce rate seems in keeping with the high moral values associated with Confucianism, and may also be explained by the general low mobility in other sectors such as employment and housing (Vogel, 1965). Another obstacle may be the scarce opportunities for women to be employed with a substantial income or to remarry after a certain age. Those factors often make women financially dependent on their husband, thus restricting their choices (Sugimoto, 1997). Recent divorce trends indicate that many modern couples see the purpose of marriage as child-rearing, financial security, or social status, rather than as the development of a husband-wife relationship. Today, increasing numbers of divorces in Japan take place after adult children's independence (e.g. their graduation from university, their marriage), or husband's retirement. In the 1990s, over 30% of all divorces occurred among couples married for over 15 years (http://www.jinjapan.org/insight/html/, 1 October 1997).

Table 2.1 Comparative divorce rate (measured as the proportion of the number of divorce cases per thousand people)

US	4.83 (1988)	West Germany	2.04 (1989)
Britain	2.86 (1989)	France	1.90 (1988)
Sweden	2.22 (1990)	Japan	1.37 (1991)

Source: Sugimoto. (1997), *An Introduction to Japanese Society*, p. 168.

Third, the abolition of the one-son succession rule also affected family relations and people's living arrangements. With the father's retirement, the house would be passed on to the eldest son according to tradition, who became the head of the household and continued to live with his older parents. However, situations such as the erosion of family traditions, decreasing birth-rates, and people's changing lifestyles and preferences have widened the choices open to people (Okazaki, 1991). Although, compared to other nations, coresiding with a married son is still a far more common arrangement in Japan (approximately 40% of total households), increasing numbers of older people live with their daughters, or second or third son, without many traditional obligations involved (Management and Coordination Agency, 1986).

Finally, the abolition of the *Ie* system started breaking down the traditional in-law relations. Disputes between a bride and her mother-in-law, which were inevitably common under an extended family, have become more overt with the erosion of family traditions. Under the new Civil code, it is no longer a duty or an obligation of the eldest son to live with his parents, or his wife to care for her parents-in-law. With the shift towards a nuclear family, marriage ties and decisions of a couple have gained priority over family lineage. With the introduction of the democratic legal system in the late 1940s, the incompatibility of a bride with her parents-in-law, especially her mother-in-law, became a common reason for divorce (Ohama, 1953). Young brides seem less tolerant towards survival of the family traditions. The abolition of the *Ie* system becomes, therefore, an important factor in many instances of contemporary divorce.

Gender Inequality

Despite the democratization of the family that has occurred, gender role differentiation between married couples still exists, and continues to shape women's position in the family. Legally, the new Civil code has removed the former restrictions on the financial independence and the rights of inheritance of the wife. Women are also given equality in grounds for divorce and in the exercise of parental power. Also, women who manage the household finances are given far more authority than traditional Confucian ideology would deem to be acceptable. In many husband-wife relationships, the status of women has been raised and the traditional gender role differentiation minimized.

Over the post-war period, urban segments have changed more rapidly, so that by the late 1940s these women had come to enjoy much freer relationships with their husband and his family than had their rural counterparts. Also, middle and upper strata families had come to accept the values and attitudes of a more egalitarian relation between husband and wife (Goode, 1963). Compared to the changes that had occurred in values and attitudes, however, changes in their behaviour or actual practice came at a much slower pace.

The modern family system, however, has not granted full gender equality to women. The majority of household chores and the task of child-rearing are still predominantly carried out by women while their husbands are engaged in paid work. Moreover, caring for older people is left mainly to women. In the mid-1980s, more than 70% of family carers for bed-ridden older people were female, and approximately a half of them were reported to be *yome* [daughter-in-law] (Figure 2.3). This figure remains high in the 1990s (Yasukochi, 1995).

Figure 2.3 Percentages of family carers for bed-ridden older people in Japan

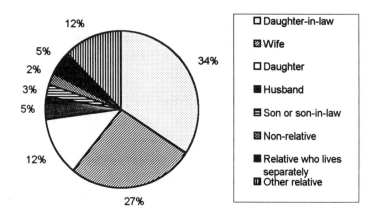

Source: Sugimoto. (1997), *An Introduction to Japanese Society*, p. 149. (The Welfare Administration Basic Survey of the Ministry of Health and Welfare, 1984).

Intergenerational Relations

Types and Pattern of Family Relations

The role and structure of family relations have various dimensions. Finch (1989) classified types of support in the family under five main headings: economic support (financial); accommodation (structural); personal care; practical support and child support; and emotional and moral support. Other scholars add further categories such as associational (contact among family members) or consensual (sharing of opinions) support (Lawton et al, 1994). Solidarity in family relations is, indeed, represented in many ways.

One form of intergenerational relations is represented structurally by accommodation, or living arrangements. Such structural aspects of family relations symbolized by coresidency is stronger in Japan than in most other industrial nations. Functional support is another noteable dimension of Japanese family relations. Helping each other in the family with daily tasks, especially older people receiving high levels of support 'up' the generations from adult children, is a typical Japanese characteristic. Economic support is another, involving the exchange of money between generations over time.

When both generations are financially independent due to income, savings, or pensions, financial support is often limited to the seasonal exchange of cash gifts in Japan. Unless the two generations live in close proximity, family contact is also likely to be limited as adult children's seasonal visits to their parents, or by telephone calls. Modern communication methods such as the telephone, faxes, and even e-mail, and private cars and public transport are able to facilitate "intimacy at a distance" (Hashimoto and Kendig, 1992).

The pattern of family support may be more demanding and frequent in Japan than in Western societies. Traditional Japanese culture seems to have more scope for structuring predictable and fair exchanges between parents and a child than is found in Western societies with long-established values of individualism (Kendig, 1989). Such strong structural and functional family relations, however, do not necessarily indicate strong emotional ties in Japanese families. The patterns of generational exchange in Japanese family life are often contradictory between comparatively low levels of affection and high levels of other support between generations.

Structural Support: Coresidency

One of the most conspicuous differences between the lives of older people in Western societies and those in Japan was the latter's preference for intergenerational living arrangements. Levy (1965) pointed out in the 1960s that even in those modernizing societies noted for joint or extended family households, most households actually consist of nuclear families. Also, Laslett and Wall (1972) have shown that this was true of pre-industrial England. The majority of people in Japan, on the other hand, used to spend their latter years living with their children, and approximately six out of ten older people aged 65 years and older still live intergenerationally (Management and Coordination Agency, 1995), while their Western counterparts usually live separately from their grown-up children. However, a recent trend in Japan has shown a shift towards more independent living, which results in an increase in the number of nuclear families as well as elderly-only households. Previously, many scholars believed that family nuclearization would advance more quickly in Japan than has actually been the case (Morioka, 1973).

Even though an increase in both the size and proportion of elderly-only households is a significant factor, the majority of older people still live with their children. Japanese society has maintained its family system for such a long time, and people generally appreciate the positive aspects of living with other generations. They place a higher value on the merits of living together with other generations as a way of sharing expenses and providing physical and financial assistance, than on the disadvantages such as generational conflicts, or the lack of privacy, independence or individual lifestyles. The following are some aspects of current and transitional coresidency.

First, more old-olds live with their children than young-olds.[5]   In 1992, only 55% of young-olds lived with their children, while as many as 61% of older people over 70 years old did so. Moreover, widows (and widowers) are more likely to be dependent on their children. According to the *1992 Basic Survey on the Life of People*, only 37% of older people over 70 years old who lived with a spouse also lived with their children, while 53% of the same age group without a spouse lived with their children (Ministry of Health and Welfare, 1992a). A spouse is likely to be the first person to rely on when assistance is required for those who are married; children would become the second source of support after the loss of a spouse.

Second, a survey conducted by the Management and Coordination Agency in 1989 showed that among four different age groups, ranging from 30 to 69 years old, younger people expressed a greater preference for living independently, compared to those in their 50s and 60s. Also, women preferred independent living more than men (Figure 2.4). As general living standards continue to improve in Japan, younger people can expect better financial security such as old-age pensions and their own savings to support themselves in retirement. Furthermore, there are changing views concerning lifestyles and families. Women used to sacrifice their middle-age life and time to look after older parents, especially their in-laws. Today, however, people are beginning to place greater emphasis on individual values, rather than on the traditional family system.

Third, in terms of residential location, the percentage of older people who live with their children increases as the size of a city's population decreases. There were a greater number of elderly-only households in big cities with populations in excess of one million than in rural areas, according to the *1992 Basic Survey on the Life of People* (Ministry of Health and Welfare, 1992a) (Figure 2.5). This may be explained by stronger traditional customs in rural areas, and also by the fact that houses of a size adequate to accommodate extended families are more available in the less populated areas. Residents of big cities often migrate from one place to another, and this migration also makes it more difficult to maintain extended family living. One study shows that in general, the older the parents, the shorter the distance from their children (Hirosima, 1987). This 1980s study concluded that some people move to be closer to their family as they age or experience a change in their personal circumstances.

Figure 2.4 Age group preferences for intergenerational living

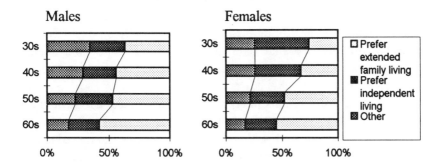

Source: Management and Coordination Agency, Japan. (1989), *Choju-Shakai ni okeru Danjo-Betsu no Ishiki no Keikou ni Kansuru Chousa [Survey on Gender Attitudes to Ageing Society]*.

Figure 2.5 Older people's living arrangements, by residential location and household type

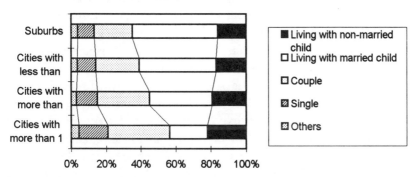

Source: Ministry of Health and Welfare, Japan. (1992), *Kokumin Seikatsu Kiso Chousa [Basic Survey on the Life of People]*, Tokyo.

Indeed, urbanization tends to lead to an increase in the number of nuclear families and to a decrease in the number of traditional extended families (Ogawa, 1992). An unwillingness to include older family members as a part of the household, however, does not simply imply a dissolution of the traditional family structure. Respect for seniority is still regarded as one of the essential virtues of Japanese society (Palmore and Maeda, 1985). The reasons for coresidency can be influenced by both traditional normative ideas and practical factors. Coresidency with older parents is most often considered an obligation or a duty for adult children living in rural areas (Hirosima, 1987). Under the *Ie* system, coresidency or sharing all assets with older parents was legally defined as well as morally obliged (Koyano, 1996). Such normative ideas are likely to continue to affect people's beliefs and behaviour, especially in rural areas where social change has had less impact on their lives.

Coresidency still retains many contemporary functional advantages. Providing safety and security to older people is one advantage of coresidency, while interaction with other age groups tends to reduce the loneliness which older people may experience through independent living. It can also allow older people to 'age in place' by helping to retain strong social contacts within the neighbourhood community and their families. For the younger urban population, coresidency can be seen as a way to achieve a better quality of life more economically. For a younger couple, this convenient, or cost-effective option includes access to housing, and child care provided by their parents, particularly useful if the younger wife is employed (Ito and Sonoda, 1994). Living in close proximity makes sharing experiences and helping between the generations more feasible with limited resources. More face-to-face contact and opportunities to help each other may strengthen other aspects of solidarity, providing an "opportunity structure" for interaction (Lawton et al, 1994) (see Chapter 6 for further policy initiatives for promotion of coresidency).

Lack of social assistance is another factor which may encourage coresidency in modern Japan. With the rapid and substantial social changes that have taken place, there coexist contradictory factors relating to the ageing population and the role of the family in Japan. While respect for older people is still regarded as a virtue, social services for older people are much less developed than in Western societies (Maeda, 1993). One of the reasons for traditionally high rates of dependency by older Japanese on their children is the lack of social systems which could have supported older people's independent living (Ito and Sonoda, 1994). There are many older people who have no choice but to coreside with their children because of inadequate financial means or a lack of social programs. The future development of a social assistance system and an improvement in social services are, therefore, likely to affect the living arrangements of older people positively. By reducing the burden for families who care for them, it may also serve to minimize their dependence on their children and ultimately help to keep older people out of institutions.

Increasing numbers of elderly-only households can be explained as a more positive shift towards independent living. First, economic development encouraged a shift to nuclear family units. Factors such as increased specialization of occupations and increased job-related geographic mobility are conducive to separate generations and the development of a nuclear family as smaller functional family units (Sussman et al, 1980).

Second, post-war industrialization improved people's living standards, and the society and its people became more affluent, compared to previous generations. The main driving force behind extended living is no longer one of survival. Self-help within the family used to be the only way of redistributing resources. The younger generation, however, has easier access to goods, services, and better quality housing than previous generations. Due to pensions, savings, and investments, many older people are in a much more favourable economic situation than previous generations and simply do not require as much financial assistance from the younger generation (Ito and Sonoda, 1994). Surprisingly, only 15% of older Japanese people mentioned children as a source of income in 1996, down from 30% in 1981, which may reflect the relative affluence of older people in recent years (Management and Coordination Agency, 1996).

Third, the rate of movement to smaller family units is partly determined by the availability and high costs of housing, and the size of newly constructed housing in urban areas. Since the late 1970s, the housing stock (the number of dwellings) in Japan had become sufficient to house the population; but there were shortages of adequate housing stocks which could accommodate extended families in urban areas. Dwelling size has decreased as the price of land has increased; this trend is especially evident within the urban inner cities (see Chapter 6). Rooms in Japanese housing used to be multi-functional. Without much fixed furniture such as beds, a dining table, or soft furnishings such as sofas, the family ate, worked, socialized, and slept in the same room. Such houses made possible the accommodation of the extended family without providing individual private rooms. Contemporary lifestyles, on the other hand, require more space and more rooms for the family, otherwise household size has to be smaller to accommodate the family in the limited space.

Finally, the most prominent explanation for the separation of older parents and their adult children may be due to people's changing views of life and family (Zenkoku Shakai Fukushi Kyougikai, 1994).   Japanese youths are growing more individualistic and self-centred, often making decisions without considering traditional values (Life Insurance Cultural Centre, 1993).   The influence of Confucian-based views on life and family is gradually decreasing over generations, and people are becoming more aware of the importance of individual lives and pursuits.   Therefore, decreasing coresidency in Japan can be attributed not only to changes in the availability of adult children, but also to changes in residential choices by both generations (Hirosima, 1987).

Functional Support: Old-Age Care

In the past, the family has been the most essential resource for assistance and security – a collective view of family obligations being the basis for survival (Hareven, 1994).   Filial piety had traditional ideological and ethical roots in Japanese people.   In modern Japan, public transfers play a significant role in supporting older people, although families still provide their dependents with many support services such as education and welfare within the household (Maykovich, 1978; Ogawa, 1992).   The relatively slow development of the welfare state has compelled the family, particularly its female members, to continue to shoulder the major burden of any welfare care necessary for other family members.   For many women, providing care for their older dependents (e.g. parents(-in-law) and a husband) remains one of the most demanding family responsibilities (see Figure 2.3).

The family-state relationship has been critical in terms of welfare provision, since a sudden change in the nature of the family and the rapidly ageing population in the post-war period had left social institutions unprepared.   The mismatch between existing (and the increasing) care needs of the older population and the adequacy of social institutions becomes further pronounced when women's social participation (predominantly, labour force participation) increases.   Indeed, adequate facilities and services for the care of older dependent people have not been developed sufficiently in Japan to fill the gap vacated by women in support roles.   Therefore, for married women, especially, entry into the labour market and the pursuit of a career have been handicapped by such underdeveloped social institutions.

For those women dubbed the 'generation in the middle,' the timing of family support such as child care and care for their older parents(-in-law) may effectively block their career development, since the years of heaviest family responsibilities are also the years most heavily invested in building a career.

The falling birth-rate and increased longevity mean that parents in modern society may have fewer children to support, but a greater burden will fall on the younger generation and existing family resources. Currently, supporting parents in their old age is a controversial issue. Since family responsibility has been largely defined legally and normatively in Japan, one confusion lies between 'duty' and 'natural feeling'. The feeling of obligation for family support is well explained in the Japanese terms *'on'* and *'gimu'* [to repay limitless indebtedness]. For instance, the debt children feel towards their parents for having suffered and sacrificed throughout their upbringing has to be reciprocated and paid back by caring for their parents in old age. For parents, therefore, having raised children earlier in life can serve as a credit for the receipt of support from them in their old age (Hashimoto and Kendig, 1992). Between generations, it is possible for the exchange to be one-way over a longer term (i.e. parents may be net 'providers' at a particular point in time because of a reasonable expectation that they may be net 'receivers' at a later date). The traditional Confucian ethics taught through Japanese education have helped to develop the responsibility for such family support into a 'good custom'.

In modern society, some younger people are more likely to interpret the norm of family support as a 'natural duty' of children rather than as a traditional 'good custom' (Kendig, 1989). In reality, with other tasks competing for their time and energies, the younger generation may even view family support more as a burden than as such a superficial idea of 'good custom'. In fact, the value shift which Japanese youth exhibit towards 'individualism' partly explained the breakdown of traditional practice. According to a recent comparative survey on youth conducted by the Prime Minister's Office in 1993, only 23% of Japanese youth aged between 18 and 24 years old were 'positively' thinking of supporting their parents in their old age, in contrast to 63% of their American counterparts (Prime Minister's Office, 1994) (Figure 2.6). The result contradicted the assumed stereotypes of the Japanese values of work, family and society (Yoshizaki, 1997).

Figure 2.6 Percentages of youth planning to support their parents (1993)

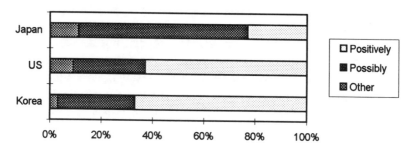

Source: Prime Minister's Office, Japan. (1994), *Sekaino Seinen tono Hikaku kara Mita Nihon no Seinen [Japanese Youth in Comparison with Youths around the World]*, Tokyo.

This shift was also observed in relation to family values, especially respect for parents. In the past, parental authority was part of a general orientation towards hierarchies between superiors and inferiors, and between seniors and juniors in all relationships in Japan (Kendig, 1989). However, Ishii et al revealed that despite such strong Confucian influence, only 31% of Japanese college students respect their parents, while 54% of American and 57% of Korean counterparts do (Ishii et al, 1994). There is no doubt that generational discontinuities are keenly felt, especially by the older generation (Lebra, 1984). Also, further increases in nuclear family households and dual-career families may alter the Japanese willingness to care for their older parents unconditionally (Maeda, 1982). As a consequence, people have started seeking alternative economic and service support from the public and market sector to assist with care in the family.

Concluding Comments

"The two of us" – an older couple answered when they were asked to define their family size in their extended family household. Even though they coreside with their son's family under the same roof, they consider themselves two different families. "No matter how close we live from each other, once our son is married, he has become an independent individual who has his own family" (*Asahi Shinbun*, 15 December 1996, p. 30).

Family formation in Japan is indeed transforming from the single conventional description of the traditional extended family of three generations. With the post-war socio-economic and legal changes that have occurred, the traditional living arrangement of coresidency is being gradually eroded, and the modern Japanese family takes various forms as witnessed by the increasing number of elderly-only households.

Many interrelated and interdependent factors have accelerated the shift away from coresidency, and the transformation of family functions. For example, the abolition of the *Ie* system, and thus, the liberation from strong Confucian doctrine, have helped to reduce people's feeling of obligation for family support. Also, women's role and position are no longer merely defined by benefits of the family. Economic independence of the older generation has also expanded their residential choices. As a consequence, older people's expectations and the actual practice of coresidency have been scaled back. Likewise, the shift away from coresidency between adult children and their older parents has made the traditional exchange of support within the household even more difficult.

In the next chapter, the process and direction of the transformation from family traditions are examined, using empirical evidence obtained from the fieldwork. It sets out to ascertain the experiences of the women and their coping strategies for such transformations. Considering the increase of elderly-only households, the next chapter examines particularly whether the shift away from coresidency is a temporary arrangement, an inevitable one due to the prevailing circumstances, or indeed, a positive choice by the women.

Notes

1   The 'bubble-economy' was characterized by rising stock values and asset prices caused by the low cost of borrowing and financial deregulation. The speculative mentality of both firms and individuals was further boosted by the growing influence of Japan's capital market and land deregulation policies, but burst suddenly when the Bank of Japan took the decision to raise the official discount rate after a period of historically low rates.

2   In this context, the working population are defined as people aged between 15 and 64 years inclusive who are engaged in paid work.

3   The term 'coresidency' is used in this book interchangeably with terms such as 'intergenerational living' or 'extended family living'.

4   Japan has its own calendar – each period of Japanese history was identified by either military government ruled by *shogun* or the regimes of successive emperors. The *Edo* period was ruled by *shogun* of the Tokugawa family.

5   In this book, the term 'young-old' refers to people from 60 years old to 69; the 'old-old' to people 75 and older. Some definitions are more detailed and specify that the term 'young-old' refers to people from 55 years old to 64; 'old' to people from 65 to 74; the 'old-old' to people from 75 to 84; and the 'super-old' to people 85 years and over (Meshida, 1991).

3   Women and Family Relations

Introduction

This chapter aims to provide an analysis of post-war family democracy from the perspective and experiences of older Japanese women. It focuses particularly on intergenerational relations, as an aspect of the transformation of family and society. As explained in Chapter 2, family nuclearization did not advance as quickly as was expected during the process of urbanization in Japan. It was also argued that the current increase of nuclear families may not be due to a substantial change in the old custom, but a postponement of coresidency (Hashimoto, 1992; 1993). Since temporary separation does not seem to be the only explanation for the recent phenomenon, the driving forces for increasing numbers of elderly-only households are examined.

The substantive ideological change taking place in people's decision-making process has also to be noted in relation to the current decline of coresidency rates. With an expansion of options and available resources in post-war society, people began expressing a greater preference for *honne* choices (Kendig, 1989), which often led them to opt for more independent living arrangements. Older women were no exception – drawing out their *honne*, however, was not an easy task in the interviewing process. Their normatively-driven answers to the questions sometimes contradicted their actual arrangements regarding housing choice and family support. Indeed, the life stories of the women in the particular cohort provide substantial insight into the transformation of the family and society through their individual perspectives, ambivalent feelings and experiences.

Characteristics of the Research Cohort

According to the Japanese calendar, each period of Japanese history had individual characteristics, marked by the regimes of successive Emperors (or *shogun* [general (=leader)] in power) (Figure 3.1).[1] The women who were interviewed in the research were born between *Taisho* 5 (1916) and *Taisho* 15 (1926). The *Taisho* period (1912-1926) followed the *Meiji* period (1868-1912) which was characterized by strong national goals (*'fukoku kyouhei'* [rich nation, strong army]) and values, and lasted for only 15 years. The distinctive social values and system of the *Meiji* period were strongly influenced by Confucian norms and the traditional *Ie* ideology, which the *Taisho*-born population inherited. The *Taisho* period was followed by the long democratizing period of *Showa* (1926-1989).

Figure 3.1 The Japanese calendar according to the successive emperors

Japanese Calendar

1		45(1)	15(1)	20		64(1)	12
Meiji		Taisho		Showa		Heisei	

Western Calendar
1868 ——————————1912——1926————1945———————————— 1989——2000

At the end of the Second World War, the women in this cohort were of marriageable age (between 18 and 28 years old). At this time, their parents or relatives followed traditional procedures to arrange their marriage. Typically, those women had no say in the selection of their partner, and simply obeyed their parents' decision. However, some women never got married, partly because there were not enough eligible men. At that time, the ratio was explained as *"one bachelor to every truck load of women"* (K.U (71)).

Married couples in this cohort produced the baby-boomer population, and raised them in a rapidly democratizing society. The post-war generation could naturally adapt to this family ideology. The same process, however, could be viewed and experienced very differently for the research cohort of the pre-war generation, which was brought up with traditional values under severe economic conditions. Sometimes, those women called themselves the *"disadvantaged sandwich generation, having experienced a 180 degree change in family systems, values, and relations after the War"* (M.H (72), T.S (76)).

Transformations to Modern Society

Social Change and Living Standards

Since levels of affluence have increased substantially in modern Japanese society, the primary reason for traditional extended family living is no longer survival or self-help. Moreover, some of the responsibilities for economic security have shifted from families to governments. With post-war economic growth, younger generations gained easier access to employment, goods and services, and a better quality of life than previous generations. Different social experiences in different age groups have created a generation gap in lifestyles and social values. Perhaps a raised living standard was one reason to reinforce individual lifestyles, and weaken the consensual (sharing of opinions between the generations in the family) and normative aspects of intergenerational ties;

> *"Young people these days don't understand what kind of food and goods we used to get with coupons right after the War. Powder soup was particularly nasty, it was hard to make bubble for washing. 'Now, it's a disposable society!', my daughter says."* (M.H (72))

> O.M (78) thought that an affluent society did not make young people value things properly. *"After the War, we suffered very much from a shortage of food and other goods. There was only one pair of boots among my four children, so three of them had to go to school barefoot. Before we bought our first black-and-white TV, we used to watch some important events like the crown prince's wedding on a street TV [a communal TV, located in a street]. Compared to our time, even young children these days have a TV each in their own room. It results in less conversation among coresident family members – my grandson spends all his time in his room."*

Financially, the retired life of older people is much easier now due to social security systems, personal investments, and savings than was the case with previous generations of older people. With the development of post-war social security systems such as pension plans, income support, or medical care, the burden of family responsibility has been reduced, and expectations of older people for family support have declined over time. Compared to western societies in which only a minority of older people receive high levels of support 'up' the generations from an adult child (Kendig, 1989), the pattern of family support may be still more demanding and more frequent in Japan. Surprisingly, only 15% of older Japanese people mentioned children as an income source in 1996, down from 30% in 1981, which may reflect the rapid improvements in the economic status of older people (Management and Coordination Agency, 1996). Again, two generations could have different perspectives upon family duties and responsibilities in this area:

> N.T (74)'s eldest son and his wife moved into her house after her spouse's death in 1989. Her son's father-in-law also passed away, so her son's wife has two widow mothers. N.T heard her saying how lucky she was since both her mother and mother-in-law were able to feed themselves (financially independent with their old-age pensions). *"It's the younger generation which thinks that I'm OK with my savings and pension. How can I expect anything from them when they say such things out loud."* She gives her adult children more financial support whenever they need it than they give her (e.g. at the birth of grand-children, or their entrance to school).

The generation which had a stronger economic status usually supported the less advantaged generation, and in the case of coresidency, contributed more to the household finances. It is evident for the research for middle to upper class families, that older parents in a position of stable health and financial security were likely to be dominant providers of family support in both coresidency and non-coresidency situations. For example, they were most likely to have accumulated assets in the form of housing. When older parents own their house, adult children could move into their parent's house without paying any rent.

A more affluent society has brought lifestyle changes. Having a separate room has, for example, become a demand even for children growing up in modern Japan. A typical small house with limited numbers of rooms and space seems problematic if coresident family members have to compromise their space and its use. Therefore, it sometimes negatively affects their decision to coreside with other generations. For older parents, moving into an adult child's house could be a different scenario from asking an adult child and his/her family to move into their house. In the former case, giving up their own house was symbolic of losing their own independence:

> M.S (82) moved to her eldest son's house after her spouse's death. *"A small house is very problematic these days. It used to be very common that all family members gathered in one room and shared all the space. But, even young children nowadays want to have their own room. In such a case [housing with limited numbers of rooms], children don't want to give up their room for a grandmother if she wants to move in."*

> Y.F (74) moved into Silver Housing[2] when she was 70. She continued to live independently. *"My son always says that I should only look at nice pottery, plates, and so on in stores, but never consider collecting anymore of them. I've already got a lot of stuff. He warned me that I would have to throw everything away if I wanted to move into his family home. His wife also likes collecting such things and has a lot already. In such a small house, I can not bring all the things I want to – it may duplicate whatever his wife has. If they choose which is to be thrown away, my son says, 'it is going to be yours, not my wife's'. It's very heartless."*

Legal Change: Abolition of the Ie System

The second point for analysis is how the legal change – the abolition of the *Ie* system – has affected older people's normative ideas regarding living arrangements and family relations. In Japan, under a patriarchal system, sons, especially the eldest son, used to have a more distinguished position and role than any other child in the family. Many informants treated their eldest son as a successor of the family, and actually passed some family duties, including ritual ones, onto him according to tradition. Care for parents in their old age appeared to be part of the 'package deal' of family succession. Having such strong normative ideas, older women faced a dilemma as to whether to follow tradition and coreside with their son or to make their own choice of living arrangement. The research revealed that increasing numbers of older women have started taking pragmatic decisions about their housing options in later life:

> T.S (77) had two sons and two daughters. Some of them lived nearby, but she lived independently in her own single-family home. Right after her spouse's death, she had completed her family duties with the passing over of *hotoke* and the title deed of the house to the eldest son. Beside

these, she would leave her savings to any of her children who would care for her in her old age if it was necessary. She also set aside some money for the cost of her own funeral. *"It does not need to be the wife of my eldest son. I would rather be cared for by my own daughters. When the time comes that I need to live with someone, I may have to have a base in my eldest son's house to respect family tradition, but want to move between my daughters' houses. But, I hope that I stay healthy to live independently as long as possible."*

Since M.S (77)'s spouse believed strongly that they had to rely on their son in later life, they packed their possessions and moved a long distance to coreside with his family in an unfamiliar neighbourhood of Kagoshima. At the last minute of leaving, her spouse was reluctant to leave his familiar neighbourhood and cried. A couple of months later, when her spouse died, she felt very lonely. There was very little conversation with her son's wife. She also found it hard to make new friends in the new town. She decided to move back and live independently in her own home. If necessary, next time, she would prefer to live with her daughters. *"I'm not obsessed by tradition anymore. I'll go wherever is good for me. I have four daughters, so I'm in a strong position. My son still insists that I move back into his house, but I don't think so. I would go to my eldest daughter's place. She is the first child of the family, so my son wouldn't be offended too much."*

The type and degree of family support and people's expectations varied according to the gender of their children. In fact, the proportion of married couples living with the parents of the husband fell steeply between 1955 and 1994, while the proportion living with the parents of the wife remained quite steady over the same period, according to data pooled from the National Survey on Family Planning (Ogawa and Retherford, 1997). This indicates that the traditional practice favouring coresidency with the eldest son has weakened considerably over time. Despite the traditions of first-son succession, the research also showed that many parents had a closer relationship with their daughters than with their sons in the areas of emotional, associational and functional family support in contemporary society:

Y.F (74) had two daughters and one son. According to custom, she had brought up her son very carefully, and always provided for him better than for her daughters. She had even trained her daughters to do the same, such as giving him the biggest piece of fish for dinner. *"Now, my daughters say cynically that I deserve good old-age care from him since I put all my care, effort, and attention to bring him up for this very purpose. But, after his marriage, I realized that I couldn't expect much from him. He has a wife. I feel much closer to my daughters who are caring and supportive in many ways. I wish I had five daughters, but no son!"*

U.Y (70) would not feel comfortable telling her son about her personal worries or family-related issues because she did not want his wife to know about them. Instead, she could be totally open with her daughter.

N.T (74) had two sons, her daughter having died at early age. Listening to her daughter-in-law's conversation with her mother, she thought that a mother-daughter relationship was wonderful. *"My relationship with my son is dull. Boys are not willing to chat much or in any great detail. He says 'good morning' when I see him in the morning, but that's all. These days, if a husband is a good person, a wife is always the one who takes the leadership in the household. So, it's possible to live with a daughter's family quite easily. I wish I had a daughter."*

Even financially, daughters were sometimes easier to consult than sons when older women in poor economic situations needed some support.

Y.F (74) believed that wives usually looked after the household finances. Her daughters had such control over household finance, and could easily allocate some cash for her when she needed it. Her son, however, always had to ask his wife's permission if the amount exceeded his pocket money. She could make *honne* requests to her own daughters, but only had *tatemae* relationship with her daughter-in-law.

As *yome* [a bride of the family], many interviewees had a very traditional relationship with their parents-in-law. *Yome*, especially that of the eldest son, used to have a prime responsibility for domestic work and matters, including old-age care, and often carrying out such tasks single-handed. Normative expectations (from whom you expect family support) and obligations (for whom you have to provide family support) varied depending on one's individual position in the family. The older women had no doubt that the duties and responsibilities of the eldest son's wife were especially demanding:

S.Y (74) became malnourished six months after her marriage. *"'Ie' which I married to had strong traditions. I, as 'yome,' was not allowed to sit at the same table with other family members for meals, even though I did all the domestic work such as cooking, washing, and cleaning. My divorced sisters-in-law were able to have meals with the family. Every morning, my mother-in-law let me quickly swallow the surface of runny porridge without any grain of rice before she stirred it up properly to serve for the family. On the way to work, therefore, I used to secretly drop by my parents' house to fill my empty stomach. I ran away from my husband's family six months later."*

T.S (76) remembered her mother-in-law's strict rules and regulations. *"When you married off your daughter to another family, she no longer belonged to your family. It was very apparent to my mother-in-law whenever she visited her own daughter's house. She always took a lunch box and tea leaves with her, so she only needed hot water [to have some tea] from her daughter's household. She was very fastidious about taking food or anything from other families."*

O.M (78) coresided with her eldest son's family. She thought that the duties of his wife were quite overwhelming. *"My son's wife has to look after her parents-in-law in their old age; she has to keep 'Ie' straight; she has to take care of ritual duties. All the family matters rest on her shoulders. Compared to her, I married the third son of the family and was excused from such duties as a wife of the family successor. Living with my son's wife, now I understand why my mother did not want me to marry the eldest son."*

N.M (75) used to live alone in a rental apartment. When she broke her hip and was discharged from hospital after two months, her only son's wife helped her with domestic chores such as laundry and cleaning at home. *"My daughter-in-law used to say, 'I'm very sorry, my husband is supposed to do this [to help you as her own child]. But, since he can't do it, I'm helping you, instead.'"*

However, almost all the interviewees felt that intergenerational relations were being transformed. Women no longer marry off legally to their husband's family. Compared with their time, old family tradition of *Ie* and bride's duties are less emphasized in younger people's modern views and values. There no longer seems any absolute parental authority over adult children in modern society. The relationship between a bride and her in-laws has also become more liberal. Different social experiences in different age groups has created a generation gap in lifestyles and social values:

> N.T (74) felt that her coresident son's wife had modern views and attitudes. *"I don't have any normative expectations for my adult children anymore. If you look around, it's so clear that no such norms [for example, 'on' (the debt children owe their parents for having suffered and sacrificed throughout their children's upbringing) should be paid back by caring for their parents in old age] exist in younger people's minds. Young people these days have totally different ideas. A bride used to adapt to her married family's 'kafuu'. I witnessed that all women in my time had to do it, and so did I. But, now, how do you say, gender equality [has taken root]?...sharing domestic tasks and so on. I wonder if it's true [that you are supposed to share domestic tasks equally between a couple]. I feel that the society has been changed a lot. We [older mothers] have to be careful not to tell a young bride to follow our 'kafuu', otherwise they would say: 'I didn't marry your family, mother! Married women these days are even able to consider keeping their maiden name!' Now, we [older parents] are the ones who have to compromise and adapt ourselves, this time, to younger people's ideas and lifestyles."*

A bride changing her surname at marriage was symbolic of her adaptation to the husband's family. Even in post-war society, this custom has carried on, it has strengthened existing social norms, and determined women's position in the family. Moreover, the family registration system itself has also determined each member's position in the family. The on-going legal amendment in the system has had a great impact upon family democracy.

Because of the generation gap in family norms and values, in-law conflicts, especially between a mother-in-law and a daughter-in-law, appeared to be a major issue in coresidency situations. When two women did not hold the same values or family customs, it was not easy to live closely together with 'other' people in the same household, sharing space, tasks and finances. Two generations often needed to compromise their space and its use to reduce tension within the home. Avoiding such conflicts or tensions may create a *tatemae* relationship between in-laws. This factor frequently influenced decisions by both older people and their daughters-in-law to coreside with each other:

> K.H (79) felt a substantial generation gap existed while she was living with her youngest son's family. Her son's young wife was not willing to

share anything with her. *"My son's wife did not talk to me for days if things did not go the way she wanted. I asked her, 'what's the matter?' But, she kept quiet."* Sometimes, when K.H helped her daughter-in-law with the washing up, it annoyed her since she considered it to be an invasion of her space and role in the household.

T.S (77) had a good relationship with her adult children. She was self-sufficient with her widow's pension and savings. Even though some of her children lived nearby, she wanted to continue her current lifestyle as long as possible. Although the spouses of her children were all nice and easy to get along with, keeping a comfortable proximity from them helped to maintain a better relationship. *"Spouses of my children are nice people, but they are 'tanin' [non-blood related 'other' people], anyway. Of course, I always feel reserved when they are around."*

K.H (73) lived with her nephew's family. In order to avoid unnecessary tension with the young family, she had been keeping her own rule. *"Whatever we are doing in the living room in the evening [i.e. having tea and cake, chatting, or watching TV], I always go up to my own room at 9 o'clock. The younger family needs their private time and space without me."*

Having different family values from the young generation, some women felt generational discontinuities. For instance, many informants frequently emphasized that the marriage bond between young couples seemed to be superseding the vertical bond or obligations between older parents and their adult children. It resulted in weakening intergenerational ties which were traditionally strong in Confucian societies:

K.H (79) used to live with her youngest son's family. He used to be strongly committed to coresiding with her when he was a child. He remained in her apartment and got married. *"Even a son like him changed when he got married. He is still very kind and caring, but as a married man he has to consult with his wife. Soon after their marriage, my daughter-in-law stopped talking to me. Whatever I asked, she didn't say a word. So, I thought that she didn't want me in the house. I decided to rent my own place."*

After the death of T.S (76)'s spouse, she moved a long distance from Miyazaki to live with her only son's family. She thought that it was the best decision, following the Confucian saying: 'When you are a child, you should obey your parents; when you marry, obey your husband; then in your old age, obey your adult children.' Six months later, her coresidency came to an end since her son's wife did not want her to live with them anymore. Her son was not willing to intervene in their conflict. She had no choice but to move into a private purpose-built retirement flat, which was located only a couple of blocks away from her son's new house. Despite the close proximity, they had little contact. *"When my son decided to marry a divorcee [his current wife], my husband was not really in favour of his marriage. The reality is nothing like younger people's ideal. In fact, it was so. Anyway, men cannot live without a woman. So, my son had to choose one woman out of two [his mother and his wife], and he chose his wife."* To a certain extent, she blamed the younger couple for disrespecting traditional family values and custom.

Social norms in relation to marriage ties, privacy, and intergenerational independence specify that older parents should not unduly interfere in or impose on the lives of their adult children and their nuclear families (Ogawa and Retherford, 1997). Power relations between generations were transformable, and there was no longer any absolute parental authority over adult children in modern society. In addition, with the fading *Ie* tradition, older parents no longer had control over the young brides.

In comparison with a standard parent-child relationship, older women's relationships with their adult *giri* [adopted] children emerged as an interesting issue. There used to be an overriding motivation for any child to repay without limit the indebtedness which they felt they owed to their parents. With a reduced degree of such family obligations among children, unconditional obligations and responsibilities towards older parents still appeared to remain strong in the case of *giri* relations:

Even though O.K (77)'s only daughter had passed away 13 years ago, her son-in-law had remained as a coresident family member. Later on, her own spouse died, and her grandson also left home to take up a job in Tokyo. It became a two-person household with her and her son-in-law. In the late 1960s when the two generations bought a house together, the parents put the down payment and paid the cost of the land, while the younger couple had a small mortgage arranged to have the house built. From the beginning, the older parents let the son-in-law have ownership of the house as part of the deal to coreside with them. Even after the situation changed, they were quite happy to take care of each other. *"My son-in-law is feeling a lot of 'giri' to me, since I looked after him and his son after my daughter's death. He feels very responsible for me. He says that he would never let me go to live in a nursing home. He would push a wheelchair for me if I became frail. It is much better to have such a caring son-in-law than your own children."*

K.H (73) and her spouse raised their nephew whose parents died when he was nine years old. She gave birth to a daughter after having taken him into the family. They were planning to send him back to his original family in a few years time. But, he insisted on staying with them. Under the ideology of '*on*' [indebtedness], her nephew had been feeling very obliged to coreside with his foster parents and look after them in their old age. This commitment was a major factor when he came to marry. As a result, his wife sacrificed much to carry on a traditional relationship with her parents-in-law, and cared for K.H's sick spouse for several years before he died.

In this particular *giri* relationship, power relations between the generations always seemed to favour the older parents, because of the nephew's strong normative ideas about being an unnecessary burden to the family. Unlike other informants, K.H (73) also emphasized the importance of normative values;

"I think that it's a good custom that children are obliged to look after their older parents in their old age. Also, a wife should be grateful to take care of her parents-in-law, since the parents are the ones who gave birth and brought up her husband." (K.H (73))

In contrast, K.H (73) did not expect or demand anything from her own and only daughter, who has other commitments – as a mother of young children and a wife of the eldest son of the family. Bringing up her own daughter was a natural duty for the parents, which she did not expect her daughter to reciprocate. Despite her normative implication in family duties, her attitudes towards her own daughter and adopted son were quite different:

K.H (73)'s demands and degree of control over the coresident couple had been very strong. She did not seem confident of receiving proper and respectful care in old age from her nephew's wife if the power of the *giri* indebtedness came to an end with her nephew's death. When her spouse died, she thought about transferring the property entirely to her nephew. However, *"if my nephew dies before me, I have nowhere to go [It is legally possible for his wife to refuse to live with her]. So, I asked to be included as a property owner, which resulted in co-ownership with my nephew's whole family. I feel protected now. "*

Cultural Identity

In contemporary Japanese society, people have started expressing their own desires and preferences, and started enjoying more freedom. Despite Westernization, however, cultural values and identity were deeply rooted in the minds of the women, which contrasted with younger people's modern views and values. The older women still had a great reluctance to express opinions and desires openly even within the family, since respecting other people's opinions and reserving one's own were regarded as virtues according to custom. In coresidency cases, therefore, the safety and security of being with other family members were usually traded off against the freedom granted by independent living. Thus, living independently allowed the women to maximize their freedom:

> A.A (72) was glad to live independently in a private purpose-built retirement flat. *"My sister lives with her son's family. Her daughter-in-law does all the cooking, but does not consider older people's tastes and preferences very much. Because she cooks a lot of Western dishes, my sister often misses plain steamed rice, which is essential as a staple of her diet in every meal. However, she does not offend her son's wife by eating out or bringing some food in. "*

Even though older people have started making their own decisions in daily life, traditional norms still played a major role in their decision-making process. A 'shame culture', which involves a deep sensitivity to social approval (Benedict, 1947), is a good example of how Japanese family values are reinforced, and lead older people to adapt traditional living alternatives. Indeed, the significant cultural identity called *sekentei* [appearance to the public] may have constrained some people's residential choices. Although Japanese society has been transformed to a great degree from the pre-war family values to more individualistic and egalitarian ones, it does not seem easy for the older women to discard their traditional norms and values:

> M.S (77) moved with her sick spouse a long distance to live with their son's family. Her spouse did not consider any other option apart from moving into the eldest son's house. However, she decided to live independently after her spouse's death. *"I don't think that I will move to*

> my son's place again. I want to live with my daughter next time, if
> necessary. In that case, it should be with my oldest daughter who lives
> in Saitama [Greater Tokyo]. She is the first child of the family, so my
> son will not lose face, even if I don't move back in his house!"

Some families were more constrained when making residential choices than
others due to their cultural identity. A choice of living arrangement
according to occupation was also common. Frequently, adult children's
participation in family business led to coresidency with their parents.
Although it depended on the type and size of business, there were practical
reasons for two partner generations to share a house (and a household)
adjoined or located in close proximity to their business. Again, keeping up
public appearances was quite important in these cases:

> N.T (74)'s eldest son and his wife moved to her single-family home
> when her spouse died in 1989. Her son had been working for the family
> business, and lived separately in rental housing having recently married.
> "Since the office was attached to our house, it seemed too big for me to
> live alone. I thought that the situation must have looked awkward to the
> neighbours. They must have wondered why I, having a son, was still
> living alone in such a big house. It did not seem right if my son
> continued commuting without moving into the under-occupied house
> next door. Both my son and I knew that it was only a matter of time
> before we started living together. It happened much earlier than we
> expected, and we could not ignore the social pressure." She wanted to
> have an independent life as long as possible until she really needed to
> live with someone.

> For O.T (72) and her spouse, it was natural to coreside with their eldest
> daughter's family since she took a *youshi* husband, who agreed to take
> over their family business. "If we had been a salaried family, 'doukyo'
> [coresidency] wouldn't have been necessary."

Shift Towards Independent Living

Coresiding as a Change of Life Cycle

Older people's styles of residential living may shift in response to a life cycle
change such as retirement, widowhood, declining or fixed sources of income,
or chronic health problems. One explanation for the rapidly increasing

number of elderly-only households over the last decade could be that most independent living by older people was temporary, until they needed some family assistance:

> M.S (82)'s eldest son asked her to move into his house when her spouse died at the age of 68. She and her spouse had been living in a rental apartment throughout their married life. She felt lucky to receive the offer. *"Nowadays, adult children don't offer their parents the chance to coreside with them. If children don't mention it, we can't ask them [to live with them]."* She had no choice but to move into his house due to her financial circumstances. If she had turned down his offer at that time, she would not have had a second chance. *"I thought it was better to move into my son's house while I was still active and able to participate in the domestic work and help my son's wife."*

> N.H (70) had worked for the local authority until her retirement. At her retirement, her eldest son and his family moved back from Yokohama to start coresiding with their parents. The feeling of obligation to live with his parents had always been in her son's mind, so he was waiting for the right time to act.

Old Age as a Burden?

Coresidency was likely to occur with the agreement of both parties. Adult children's financial and functional ability, and their availability and willingness to support older parents also seemed prerequisites to the formation of extended family households. For many informants, having children still meant having secure carers in old age. However, with other competing tasks such as paying off mortgages or their own children's education, supporting older parents could no longer be the first priority of adult children:

> Although both Y.M (76)'s son and daughter lived in their single-family home in the same city, she remained alone in fully-subsidized rental housing, which was damp and old with a leaking roof. She felt miserable to think about her housing situation and how other people thought about her. Her daughter used to ask her to move into her house. *"But, now my grand-daughter got divorced, and moved back into the house with two children. So there is no space for me anymore, and my daughter is devoting her time to looking after them."*

T.S (76)'s expectations were heavily let down when coresidency with her only son's family did not work out. *"I have no expectation whatsoever to receive long-term care from my only son's wife. The less I expect from my child, the better, anyway. I won't be disappointed if they [her son and his wife] don't care for me. My only wish is that when I die, my son would pick up my bones after the cremation of my corpse.*[3] *I hope that he would at least do that. In that sense, I'm in a better situation than my friend who is still wondering who will pick up her bones."*

O.T (71) lived with her unmarried 46-year-old daughter in her own home. *"Living with her is good for me to reduce my loneliness, especially at night. But, [it's] not good for her. It is a pity that she is going to be alone after I die. I'm encouraging her to move near her sister's house in Tokyo when it happens."* She thought that the unmarried status of her daughter was unfortunate. She did not value her daughter's other strengths, such as her career or social network.

Independent living in later life was also chosen by those women who had devoted themselves to other family members throughout their life according to traditional customs. Almost all informants had accepted the increasing individuality of the younger generation, and were unwilling to burden them with the responsibilities of care in old age. Through their experiences, the women came to resist the idea of relying on their adult children and becoming a burden to them. If they did, it also meant for the women losing their own independence and freedom. The collective views suggested that in their minds, normative expectations existed on a superficial level, such as the necessity of keeping public appearances. In actual practice, many wished to enjoy their own lives and independence:

K.H (79) had single-handedly provided old age care for her bed-ridden spouse at home for 10 years. Since her children witnessed her struggle, she was quite confident that her children would not abandon her. However, she did not want them to repeat what she had done – looking after their old mother for a long time before her death. She did not want to be a burden to the family. Since her experience of coresidency with the youngest son's family was not successful, she chose to live in a public home for older people. She hoped that none of her children was offended with her decision, because people may have thought that they 'dumped' her in a home. If she became sick, she would rather go to hospital, not to her children's home.

A.A (72) lived independently in a private purpose-built retirement flat, away from her children. Three years ago, she found that she had cancer, but she decided not to tell her children about it. *"Unless we live close to each other, it is better to keep it secret. Since they have their own lives, I don't want to bother them with things which they could do nothing about. I want to die quickly, you know, 'go to bed one night, and not wake up the next morning'."*

M.S (77) had one son and four daughters, but lived independently in her own home. *"My children will not let me go and live in a nursing home. They say that for what purpose I suffered and sacrificed myself to bring them up, if I can't rely on them later on."* She expressed her preference to move into her first daughter's house in Saitama when she needed assistance in the future. However, her *honne* statement was: *"Although I say I prefer moving into my daughter's house [to a nursing home], I don't really want to do that, either. I'm so used to living alone and doing things I feel like doing. I'm hoping to die easily."*

The collective views of the older women was that they wished to die quickly and easily, without the onset of senile dementia or becoming bed-ridden for a long time, or becoming a burden to their adult children.

Choice! It's Great to be Independent

To a certain extent, an increase in elderly-only households reflected older people's growing preferences for independent living. Explanations for this recent trend included the increased geographic mobility of younger people, the economic independence of older people, and inadequate housing for intergenerational living in urban areas. However, the main reason for the increasing separation of older parents and adult children may be due to people's changing views of life and family over generations. Living independently certainly allowed the older women to avoid unnecessary conflicts from the younger generation, to enhance the importance of their individual life and pursuits, as well as to maximize their freedom:

M.S (77) lived independently in her own home. She enjoyed living independently because of the freedom. *"This morning, I got up, had breakfast, and went back to sleep again. If you lived with your family, you could not sleep in. You have to get up early enough to have breakfast with them. If other family members go to work or school, how can you be lazy and stay in bed."*

> When A.A (72) visited her son's house, she was very offended to see him taking a garbage bag out in the morning. His wife asked him to do it, and it seemed to be one of his domestic routines. *"I never let my boys do domestic chores, nor let them help me in the kitchen, let alone taking a garbage bag out! I would never be able to live with the modern family."*

Starting coresidency through a change in personal circumstances such as retirement, widowhood, ill-health, and financial circumstances seemed relatively difficult since both generations or households had already established separate lifestyles. Many informants, therefore, expressed their preference to be independent from adult children, to remain in their own house, in their own community with social networks, even after significant life cycle changes. The research revealed that many were in favour of independent living, yet were ambivalent towards receiving family support in old age. The majority of the informants resisted the idea of becoming a burden to their adult children, and losing their independence and freedom:

> S.Y (74) had experienced living with her sister and unmarried nephew. Currently, she lived in a rented unit provided by the Housing Corporation on her little pension. Her nephew had been asking her if she wanted to move back into their house. *"Well, I'm living alone in comfort now. Even though we are blood-related sisters, I have 'enryo' [reservations] towards her. We sometimes have different opinions. It gets troublesome, so we'd better not live together. My nephew says that I would be able to save a lot of money by not paying rent. And, coresidency is better if I become sick. But, you know, I don't like feeling constrained."*

Many stressed the importance of being emotionally independent from adult children. In other words, it was one of the coping strategies for those to prevent disappointment from unfulfilled normative expectations. Some women were able to adjust to the value shift more successfully than others:

> U.Y (70) lived independently from her children in her own house. Her social experience as a nursery teacher made her realize that the older generation had to change their attitudes and beliefs. *"People with social experiences are more aware of the change, and able to accept or respond to the transition. It must be harder if you had only lived within the family for all your life."*

After her divorce, Y.F (72) had been living independently with her own income, and then with a pension. At her present age, she had no intention of depending on her only son. *"It was more than enough for me that my son had occasionally come to see me in the hospital where I stayed for three months. My daughter-in-law also visited me in the hospital to provide personal care for me. I have my own life and they have theirs. It is too much to ask my son, who is bringing up his own children, to care for me at the same time."*

Concluding Comments

The collective voice of the older women represented changing family traditions and social norms over the post-war period. The authority which older parents used to hold over their children has been reduced with the abolition of the *Ie* system. Thus, apart from the unique *giri* relationship, women in the family have been significantly liberated from traditional roles and positions to pursue family obligations. For the women, receiving care in old age was viewed as a burden on their children rather than as support they could expect. Indeed, the newly-found family democracy inevitably transformed family relations, and widened the generation gap. Despite the remaining *Ie* tradition, many women expressed closer ties with their own daughters than sons, but weakening intergenerational ties over the marriage bond between young couples.

Many of these women were still caught between traditional norms (cultural values) and their own preferences in decision-making, which sometimes constrained their residential choices. However, changing family traditions and relations have substantially transformed their residential choices. Overall, the research has highlighted that either through choice or constraint, traditional extended family living has shifted towards more independent living alternatives for the older women concerned. Increasing numbers of women enjoy living independently, thus avoiding potential generational conflicts. The decreasing rate of coresidency has created difficulties in continuing the traditional exchange of family support. In contemporary Japan, family resources have to be discounted in the mixed economy of welfare.

In the next chapter, changing family relations are further analysed in the context of the development of the post-war welfare state. The role of the family in the Japanese welfare state is reviewed, along with how the development process has influenced the position and status of women in the family and society.

Notes

1   Some periods between *Kamakura* (1192-1333) and *Meiji* (1868-1912) were ruled by *bakufu* [military government] under *shogun* in power.
2   Purpose-built rental housing for older people, funded and operated by the local authority.
3   In Japanese funerals, it is an important ritual for family and close friends to pick up the bones with long chopsticks after a cremation.

4 The Japanese Welfare State in Transition
'From Feudalist to Post-Bubble Capitalist State'

Introduction

Japan's post-war economic growth has been remarkable.[1] Japan became one of a handful of non-Western nations that was both democratic and industrialized with an established social security system within a relatively short period of time. On the other hand, its development of welfare programs was often regarded as 'lagging behind' its significant economic achievement. Criticism was found in both Western and Japanese literature that Japan had gained post-war economic success partly at the sacrifice of welfare (Lee, 1987; Nakagawa, 1979; Rudd, 1994). For instance, when measured as a proportion of GDP, public expenditure on welfare in Japan has been relatively low compared to other industrial nations. According to ILO reports on the Costs of Social Security, most industrial nations were spending two to three times the Japanese rates in the 1960s and 1970s. Although a significant improvement has been made since then, current Japanese rates are still considered to be low – approximately equivalent to the average for OECD countries in the 1960s (Table 4.1). Certainly, the imbalance between the rapid economic growth and the relatively slow development of a comprehensive welfare state, and differences in Japan's social policy development from Western nations makes it all the more interesting to analyse.

The relatively low proportion of expenditure on welfare as a percentage of GDP does not necessarily indicate, however, that Japan has been a welfare-poor nation. Within the concept of welfare pluralism, the richness of welfare provision in Japan can be illustrated on the basis of strengths of other sectors, including traditional family resources, the role of the market, accompanied with post-war development of occupational

59

welfare.   Nevertheless, changing family tradition, social values and a restructuring of the employment system as well as rapid demographic change necessitate adjustment to existing systems.   As we approach the twenty-first century and new economic pressures come to bear, the welfare state in the post-bubble era is also facing an important turning point.

Table 4.1 Social security expenditure as a percentage of GDP (%)

	1970	1980	1983	1990
Japan	5.3	10.8	12.0	14.0
UK	13.7	17.3	20.5	20.5
Sweden	18.6	31.9	33.3	35.2

Sources: ILO, The Cost of Social Security, 1981-1983 (for the 1970, 1980, 1983 data);
        Japan Statistics Yearbook, 1990 (for Japan, 1990); UK National Accounts 1991,
        HMSO (for UK, 1990); SCB Statistisk Arsbok for Sverige, 1992 (for Sweden,
        1990) (Gould, 1993).

In addition, the process of welfare state development has raised many issues. The conventional model of the welfare state usually assumes services such as social security,[2] health care, education, housing, and personal social services. Since education and health services including the public insurance scheme were developed relatively universally and comprehensively in post-war Japan, the analysis in this chapter concentrates on particular elements of welfare services, such as social security and personal care services. This chapter focuses particularly on the way in which the structure and nature of the Japanese welfare state have reflected and determined the roles and position of women in the family and society. It is often said that institutions such as the welfare state shape contemporary forms of social stratification. In Japan, as in most industrial nations, the target provision as well as an absence of services in some areas of welfare state may have served as driving forces to create inequalities and new social divisions in the family and society. Taking various welfare services as examples, the process and causes of creating such inequalities between genders, among families as well as individuals are investigated. Finally, new policy directions are analysed in the context of current social, economic and demographic changes.   A challenge to maximizing available resources and reducing inequalities is considered in relation to the transformed relationships among various sectors in the welfare state.

Defining the Welfare State and Its Structure

Despite some scholars' attempts at creating a typology of welfare states (e.g. Esping-Andersen, 1990; Goodman and Peng, 1996; Jones, 1993), the concept remains ambiguous and pluralistic in its meaning since each nation has its own welfare regime. Therefore, the purpose of this section is not to provide one concrete definition of a welfare state, but to provide a framework in which the regime of the Japanese welfare state can be analysed and investigated in comparison with other industrial nations.

What do we mean by a 'welfare state'? First, a welfare state is certainly one form of the state, a distinct set of institutions or organizations, which represents civil society and economy. Historically, the original concern of the state has been the maintenance of public order and the defense of its territory against foreign attack (Rose, 1986). The state's role in industrial nations as a welfare producer came rather late in response to social needs (e.g. public health) and problems (e.g. disease, social unrest) which were created by major incidents such as the Industrial Revolution, the Great Depression, and war. In this rather simple definition, the welfare state is considered as part of the state apparatus involving the provision of social security and services (Cochrane, 1993); distributing goods and services which satisfy citizens' basic needs and allow social protection as a safety net. In theory, it is implicitly assumed that the welfare state redistributes income and wealth in favour of the poorer and needy groups within society (The Dictionary of Human Geography, 1994).

Second, following the above definition, one argument stresses that it represents a particular stage in the development of society (Shiratori, 1986). This definition sees the welfare state not in terms of its role or function, but as a conception of state structure. In the process of social development, a particular type of society emerges, with material abundance resulting from the great expansion of production together with freedom and tolerance, which are caused by political developments (Shiratori, 1986). This particular type of society enlarges the capacity of the state, particularly in assuring the material needs of its citizens. In this interpretation, because such a welfare state is defined as having an inevitable connection with affluence and civil liberty, it is only possible in a developed capitalist society.

The third and most critical point of the argument is that the welfare state, as a set of social and economic policies, is also, and always has been, a system of social stratification (Esping-Andersen, 1990; Taylor-Gooby, 1991). Welfare states are key institutions in the structuring of the social order by, for example, redistributing income to reduce poverty in society. Instead of shaping the society and helping to achieve equality among people in the society, the nature of welfare states may, in fact, create and reinforce social divisions such as class, age discrimination and gender roles. For instance, the education system affects an individual's mobility chances and may create class divisions. Setting a retirement age in the labour market usually excludes older people from paid work opportunities. The male breadwinner family model, which historically shaped many welfare states, also reflects and reinforces gender roles in the family (Lewis, 1992). More recently, the organization of social services has played a role in creating a gender division in a nation's employment structure. Sweden, which has produced a social welfare-led post-industrial employment structure, represents a case in point (Esping-Andersen, 1990). Here, the growth of the female labour force was concentrated in the public sector, which thus resulted in a female-biased social-service sector. This issue is further investigated in the context of the development of the welfare state in Japan with particular reference to its effects on individuals' lives in old age, and its future direction.

Reviewing the structure of a welfare state gives us a better understanding of its composition, and the complex and changing pattern of relationships between different welfare producers. Since the state is not the sole institution to provide welfare in a society, in most industrial nations welfare usually derives from a multitude of sources (Mishra, 1990; Rose, 1986). If there are multiple sources rather than a single monopoly provider, the total welfare in a society is likely to be greater and its quality to be enhanced. Ideally, the strengths of each producer can compensate for limitation of the others by effective intersectoral combinations and networks of the producers (Evers, 1993; Rose, 1986). A much greater variety of services from which users can choose is likely to be available (Johnson, 1993); and it could allow for more democratic participation more efficiently while still protecting social justice (Evers, 1993). This approach is called *welfare pluralism,* or *the mixed economy of welfare,* and typically involves three major sectors as welfare producers: the state, the market and the family.

In most modern societies, the state has a major role in providing the major welfare goods and services desired in a society by income redistribution, medical care, education, or commitment to full employment. The state in social democratic countries, such as Sweden in particular, has a dominant role as a welfare provider. Such a state is committed to unusually strong and comprehensive social rights, built on universalistic principles. Also, it is a very service intensive welfare state with maximum employment for both men and women (Esping-Andersen, 1990; 1997). Since a state's spending commitment for welfare is high, a substantially high level of taxation is inevitable.

The second sector is the market, both private and profit-oriented enterprises. This sector can be defined in two ways: so-called occupational welfare in which an employer provides for the employees; and welfare industry in which welfare goods and services are produced within the market economy. Its role has shifted greatly in some modern societies under privatization schemes and new processes of regulation and deregulation. Governments in Britain and the United States in recent years have allowed more scope for the private sector to provide welfare, and have reduced the scope of the public sector (Mishra, 1990). Japan is not an exception to this trend of the late 20th century. In post-war Japan, a relatively affluent egalitarian society, the middle classes insure themselves mainly in the market (e.g. the high home ownership rates; the world's highest purchase rates of private health / life insurance schemes). A growing middle class in Japan results in the relative absence of demand for public action that may arise in societies where social disorganization leads to the creation of an underclass of multiply-deprived people. However, in a country where the market is the dominant source of welfare provision, access to welfare depends on income as well as needs. Such a system emphasizes equity (i.e. contractual fairness) over equality (i.e. redistribution) (Esping-Andersen, 1997). In this scenario, the role of the state becomes minimal and the family, rather than individuals, remains responsible for their own welfare.

Third, the family or households, which was absent from Titmuss' (1963) classic 'threehold division of welfare' into state, fiscal, and occupational provision, completes the structure of the conventional welfare state. Indeed, welfare is measured not only in monetary terms of the state and the market, but also in relation to non-monetarized (unpaid) welfare producers. Given that women are usually dominant producers in the informal sector, consideration of informal care in the welfare state is crucial to any understanding of women's position in the family and society (Lewis, 1992). The role of the family as a welfare producer is explicitly counted in traditional societies (e.g. 'Confucian' and 'Catholic' based countries). In Japan, for example, it has been argued that traditional virtues of family, community, and work ethics bring true welfare with less government intervention, and thus avoid the dependency and cold bureaucracy of the Western welfare states (Campbell, 1992). In fact, much welfare has been produced by non-waged housewives there, while overestimating the substitutive role to be played by the public sector. With changing family traditions and socio-economic systems in a modern society, however, access to such support is increasingly problematic and unequal and its quality varies (Evers, 1993). Overall, changing family traditions and thus changing levels of family contribution to welfare in society will lead to a very different scenario in future public policies.

In addition, the voluntary sector, private but non-profit organizations, plays an increasingly important role in this arena. Although this sector has been neither very active nor well-established in Japan compared with such countries as Britain, its potential is highly regarded as alternative welfare service providers to these existing sectors (*Asahi Shinbun*, 22 December 1997, p. 4). In theory, this sector, especially in the pluralist approach, can decentralize the existing conventional centralized production system of welfare to a certain degree; decrease the power and the cost burden of the state; and achieve more cost-effective and better quality service delivery (Shiratori, 1986; Svetlik, 1993). Also, since declining traditional family support requires substitute forms of social welfare services in Japan, it may lead to the useful reorganization of available human resources. Total welfare in a society is a sum of these sectoral provision.

Japan in Welfare Regime Models

Welfare regimes vary according to national and cultural values, resources, socio-economic situations and types of government. The proportion of welfare goods and services produced by each of the sectors also varies among nations. For example, in terms of national values, the Swedes are said to have a more positive and trusting evaluation of state activity than Americans, whereas the Japanese value the family more (Rose, 1986). Indeed, the characteristics, similarities and differences of welfare states attracted comparative policy researchers to classify them into various welfare regime models. The inclusion of Japan, an East Asian country, in such comparative analysis is increasingly common (Esping-Andersen, 1990; 1997; Heidenheimer et al, 1983; Mishra, 1990; Taylor-Gooby, 1991). In most cases, however, analysis has sought to fit Japan into one of a variety of existing welfare regime models conceptualized from a Western framework rather than examining it in its own terms (Goodman and Peng, 1996). Since it does not often sit comfortably or perfectly in given regime models, a compromise of the deviations results in calling the Japanese welfare state 'unique', an 'exception' or 'hybrid'. Hence, continuous attempts find some aspects of the Japanese welfare state similar to various Western regime models. According to the most debated classification of Esping-Andersen (1990), Japan was classified in the Eurocentoric 'corporative-conservative' regime model with Germany and Britain, in which social rights are based on employment and contributions. The Catholic influence on the family and community dependency in this regime is usually replaced with Confucianism when it applies to the Japanese welfare state. Also, the strong role of the corporate sector through established occupational welfare in Japan encourages similarities to be drawn with the 'liberal' welfare regime model (Esping-Andersen, 1997). As in the US, large and even medium-sized Japanese firms have been substantial and comprehensive social welfare providers in terms of health care, corporate pensions and housing. If the gender bias in the labour market structure is ignored, Japan's formidable commitment to maximum and full employment seems to also resemble the 'social democratic' model. According to Jones' (1993) debate in the Western context, the Japanese welfare state exhibits conservative corporatism without Western-style worker participation; subsidiary without the Church; solidarity without equality; and *laissez-faire* without libertarianism. Considering such combined elements of different regime models, a new typology of welfare states emerges. Since the establishment of the welfare state in other East Asian countries such as Korea and Taiwan has been largely based on the Japanese model, a grouping as 'Confucian welfare state' or 'American-Pacific welfare model' is increasingly popular in academic debates (Goodman and Peng, 1996; Jones, 1993).

Welfare states in various regime models have been transforming hand-in-hand with a nation's demographic, social and economic change. Thus, the mixed economy of welfare is thought of not as a unitary structure, but as a complex and changing pattern of relationships among the sectors. In recent years, with an increasing cost burden due to demographic change, a shift away from the pre-eminence of the state in the overall scheme of welfare has become inevitable in many industrial societies (Mishra, 1990). The crisis of the welfare state in the West during the 1980s especially drove many governments, including Britain and the US, to encourage their citizens to shift the dependence from the state's direct welfare provision to the market, the voluntary sector and households. This involved encouragement to join private pension and health schemes, and the (re)establishment of the family as welfare provider (Rudd, 1994). In a sense, the shift of some welfare states in the West is moving closer to the Japanese model. Certainly, the politics of welfare is now very much a politics of shifting costs from one sector to another (Mishra, 1990; Rein and Rainwater, 1986), and of more fragmented and complex patterns of provision. In Japan, where the emphasis of the state was originally minimal, such a shift is also taking place to create a new balance and mechanism of the post-bubble era. Since the Japanese welfare state is still in the process of evolution, the analysis of such transformation will be returned to at the end of this chapter.

The Development of State Initiatives on Welfare

Historically, Japan's welfare systems originated in mature Western welfare models such as those in England and Germany. The first recognized social security law, *Jyukkyu Kisoku*, introduced in 1874, was based on the Poor Law in England (1601); and health insurance in 1922, the first social insurance system, originated in the German system which was developed by Otto Bismarck in the 1870s (http://www2.nttca.com:8010/infomofa/socsec/maruo/, 1 February 1998). The Ministry of Health and Welfare was founded in 1938. The first pension system for workers was then introduced in 1941. However, evidence of the existence of a welfare state was shown in literature in the earlier *Edo* period (1603-1867). For example, a story about a doctor, nicknamed '*Akahige*,'[3] helping poor sick people in the state-funded institution, *Koishikawa Youjousho* in the 1720s (which lasted for the rest of *Edo* period) was based on a true story. The story proved that besides exchanging informal welfare within the family and community, there was a public institution providing medical care to a small needy group in much earlier years than is generally academically recognized.

   The development of contemporary public policies for welfare in Japan almost parallels Europe after the end of the Second World War. The development involved several phases. During the first 10 years, welfare development coincided with the post-war economic reconstruction. Due to the US occupation, the Americans' traditional emphasis on poor relief and personal social services was dominant (Lee, 1987). The Japanese approach was, however, to start from existing levels, and to expand coverage by adding separate programs incrementally, while maintaining prior schemes.

The period between 1955 and 1969 was identified as the second phase. Although the Japanese government had not promoted an ideology about itself as a 'welfare state', national bureaucrats drafted the legal guarantees for welfare that promised a safety net of public provided social security, such as pension and health insurance (Anderson, 1993). In a sense, the establishment of the systems of 'health insurance for all, and pensions for all' in 1961 marked the beginning of a welfare state. Although the rapid economic growth during 1950s and 1960s made it possible to catch up with Western societies, social security, working conditions and living standards remained at a relatively low level (Maruo, 1986). Consequently, popular opposition arose to demand improved welfare guarantees. By the mid-1960s, citizens' movements and local opposition groups (e.g. the student movement, a growth of left-wing parties) advanced platforms for more comprehensive welfare benefits securing health, education and retirement benefits.

The 1970s was a dramatic decade for the Japanese welfare state with increased public pressure on this arena (Goodman and Peng, 1996; Tabata, 1990). Previously, government priority had been on economic growth and industrial development. In 1973, seeking more welfare and quality of life, Prime Minister Tanaka Kakuei moved to introduce '*Fukushi Gannen*' [Welfare Year One], and referred to the ambitious transition of state priority from economic growth to welfare. As a result, the rate of the social security budget in the fiscal year 1973 was raised by 28.8%. Initially, the Prime Minister introduced national laws for child allowances for education, a Medicare bill for retired people, and increased pension benefits. Unfortunately, the momentum of the welfare reform did not last long. In the same year, after the passage of the legislation, the Tanaka government's economic policy eventually went bankrupt due to exorbitant land price inflation, the upheaval of the international monetary system, and most of all, the first oil crisis in 1973 (Tabata, 1990). The unemployment rate rose threefold between 1975 and 1985, resulting in an increase in welfare expenditure. The low economic growth rate changed the attitude and enthusiasm of the government on this issue. The slogan of 1973 was gradually replaced by 'Reconsider welfare', 'Welfare state disease', or

'Japanese style welfare state' (Lee, 1987).   This policy direction was enforced further, when Prime Minister Ohira Masayoshi addressed *'Nihon-gata Fukushi'* [Japanese style welfare society] in his speech at the Japanese National Diet in January 1979:

> *"I would like to build up a welfare society in the following way while retaining a traditional Japanese spirit of self-respect and self-reliance, human relations which are based upon the spirit of tolerance and the traditional social system of mutual assistance. I should like to add the public welfare system to a fair degree to them."*   (Shiratori, 1986)

'Self-reliance' largely meant re-establishing traditional practices of mutual aid within the family, local communities and workplace. The idea was to avoid following the path of Western welfare states towards public welfare dependency and instead to only use public assistance to supplement welfare provided by other sectors (Rudd, 1994). The concept of welfare was again shifted back to individual responsibilities. It can be said that this policy formed the foundation of the contemporary welfare state in Japan.

During the 1980s a call for the re-examination of welfare schemes came to prevail, and a number of important revisions were carried out. For instance, in order to control social spending, the government proposed to reduce entitlements (e.g. single mothers' entitlement to benefits) and limit pressure for increased public expenditure at a time when the economy was growing even more slowly (Maruo, 1986). In his inaugural speech in 1982, Prime Minister Nakasone Yasuhiro re-emphasized developing "a traditional family oriented welfare state which was different from so-called western-style welfare states". The important point here was defining the 'Japanese-style welfare state' on the premise of "the stable family and firms supporting an individual life, and the state being the last resort" (Osawa, 1993). The Nakasone government, in close co-operation with big business and advisory councils, moved to reform National Health Insurance and to restructure the public pension system. In combination with privatization efforts for national rail and telecommunication sectors, however, the Nakasone efforts to reform welfare entitlements did not significantly retrench from earlier commitments. Furthermore, the rapid societal ageing and increasing demands of the older population were gradually becoming issues concerning future resources. In response, at the end of the 1980s, just before the bubble economy burst, the government promulgated *'Kourei-sha Hoken Fukushi Suishin Jukka-nen Senryaku'* or 'ten-year Gold Plan' for the development of health and welfare services for older people. The emphasis was given to a staying-put option with various community care facilities and services reflecting older people's wishes and preferences. Again, it implicitly redefined the family role, shifting responsibility back to the family to take advantage of Japan's high coresidency rates.

Occupational Welfare: Myth of its Benefit and Equality

As in many other societies, the origins and development of the Japanese welfare state were determined by critical choices made by politicians, bureaucrats and economic leaders during the post-war transitional period; uniquely, from feudalism to democratic capitalist society (Rudd, 1994). Throughout the slower economic growth experienced over the last couple of decades, government policies led to the formation of a contemporary welfare state – the residual model – with a shift back to a relatively small state and a larger role played by households and the market sector. A small state in this context, however, only refers to the direct provision of statutory welfare. Since the state role is not only providing the direct services but also determining or influencing the socio-economic mechanism through policies, regulations and subsidies, public intervention has played a significant part in shaping the socio-economic system in Japan (e.g. housing supply [see Chapter 6], 'administrative guidance').[4] Indeed, the state and industrial relations are rather unique in Japan. Government ministries are in charge of fostering and, at the same time, regulating individual industries. This is most obvious in relation to the industrial policies of the Ministry of International Trade and Industry (MITI), with its guidelines and industrial laws, and can also be found in the banking and finance sector (Schaede, 1996). In relation to welfare, one example is the productive welfare policies: preventing unemployment through state intervention rather than paying unemployment allowances (http://www2.nttca.com:8010/infomofa/socsec/maruo/, 1 February 1998). For instance, in the 1960s, when structural changes in the economy badly affected the coal mining industry, the government implemented a comprehensive range of measures to help the miners find new jobs: removal allowances were given; training programs with allowances were established; and public works and redevelopment projects were created (Gould, 1993). Such policies have also been implemented more recently to cope with other industrial restructuring, particularly redundancies in the steel industry.

Compared to the state-oriented Scandinavian models, in terms of direct welfare provision, Japan is a good example of how the market/private sector and households can do without high levels of public provision, yet still have the majority of the population that is well educated, healthy and secure in old age (Mishra, 1990; Rose and Shiratori, 1986). The market has been playing an important role as a welfare producer, by funding pensions and retirement benefits through corporate employers, providing health care through partial payment by patients, and offering education through a large private university system. Schools commonly provide extra curricula tuition for younger pupils in Japan (Maruo, 1986). Among these, occupational welfare, or company-sponsored benefits, was developed due to the lack of comprehensive welfare provision by the state in periods of rapid economic growth. Thus, some of those benefits were seen as complements, if not substitutes for public welfare provision (Hall, 1988). In terms of its variety, service provision ranged widely from statutory requirements such as unemployment insurance, pension schemes and health insurance to company housing, retirement allowances, collective bargaining agreements (e.g. canteen meals, travel passes, petrol allowance), and medical care (e.g. company health clinic, annual health check). Some large firms also provided employee's families with allowances and gifts. For example, the education of an employee's child was supported through educational loans, and even the maintenance of a dormitory in Tokyo "for those children of employees attending universities or cram schools preparing for university entrance exams" (Dore, 1973).

Interestingly enough, post-war occupational welfare was developed with the traditional paternalistic regard in mind. If we look at Japanese society in terms of the emergence of a social fabric that reinforces the importance and relevance of traditional values, it is not surprising to observe the tendency to look upon the workplace as an extension of the family and primary groups (Takahashi and Someya, 1985). The same cultural ideology of the households was applied to the workplace and produced the 'three national treasures' of '*shuushin-koyou*' [lifetime employment], '*nenkou-joretsu*' [seniority system] and 'enterprise unionism' based on an implicit contract between an employer and the employees (Anderson, 1992). The lifetime employment system made firms principally responsible for keeping their employees in full employment. The employers' commitment also created one of the major occupational benefits, retirement allowance, which was often equivalent to one month's salary for every year employed. Obviously, many Japanese firms placed higher values on the advantages of welfare provision during periods of rapid economic growth. They believed that welfare provision improved a worker's morale and loyalty to a firm, and increased corporate identification, which led to higher productivity (Dore, 1973). Dore (1987) also argued that on several counts the community model firm was superior to the company law model firm: innovation, efficiency, competitiveness, the quality of life and kinds of satisfaction it delivered to those who worked in it were better defined. This form of welfare may have been seen as a necessary cost for the maintenance of the management system as mutual benefits between the employer and employees. Also, by raising such social wages, it managed to keep cash wages low (Hall, 1988).

On the other hand, the myth of such excellence in Japanese occupational welfare provision has been also highlighted. With the exception of some high-cost benefits such as health insurance and retirement schemes, Japanese enterprises mainly offered an extensive range of low-cost benefits. The provision of welfare by the firm was not exclusive to Japan, nor was the Japanese firm particularly generous in its provision (Hall, 1988). When compared with Western firms in Britain and the US, welfare provision was often seen as 'fringe benefits' and, frequently regarded as the preserve of higher paid employees – evident by the way in which such benefits were taxed. In Japan, they were more likely to be part of a 'total package' available for all employees (Hall, 1988). The quality of welfare also remains in question. Even though some large firms such as Hitachi still provide their first-year recruits with a shared dormitory room (e.g. two people sharing a 6 *tatami*-mat-room[5] in the late 1990s) as company housing, the quality of some benefits seems to lag behind the contemporary needs and generally accepted standards of living.

Overall, a critical point is that these benefits tended not to be distributed on a universal basis. Within the system, employees with major large firms benefited much more than those with small firms (Table 4.2). Although not strictly comparable, the more recent figures suggested that if anything the gap between small and large firms had grown especially in health-related and retirement schemes since the mid-1970s (Gould, 1993; Osawa, 1993). According to the *1991 Japan Statistical Yearbook*, retirement allowances per employee were five times higher in the largest firms than in the smallest, and non-statutory welfare was four times as high, while labour costs in total were only 70% greater. Furthermore, temporary workers, who accounted for 10% of employees, did not benefit from the same range of services as did their regular counterparts (Dore, 1973). In fact, one reason why employers prefer to use more casual labour, usually female workers, is to reduce fringe benefits costs payable. There were also major differences in provision among various industries and by gender. In 1973, welfare costs as a percentage of pay ranged from 9.1% in the publishing industry to 13.1% in metals, and 22% in the mining industry (Gould, 1993). Also, because of the diversification of women in the labour force, income differences among female workers are generally greater than among male workers (Sugimoto, 1997). For women of the same age and length of service to a firm, the wage differences in small firms and in big firms is greater than for men in the same categories.

Table 4.2 Cost of occupational welfare in Japan (1983)

Firm Size	Total Labour Cost	Retirement Allowance	Statutory Welfare	Occupational Welfare
5,000+	439	21.1	31.2	18.0
1,000-4,999	389	15.5	28.7	11.0
300-999	328	11.5	25.3	7.0
100-299	291	8.8	22.8	5.6
30-99	251	5.8	21.7	5.6
All Firms	339	12.3	25.8	9.4

Note: thousand yen per employee per month

Source: Nihon Chingin Kenkyu Centre. (1985), *Shunki Chingin Kosho Shiryo [Spring Wage Negotiation Data]*, pp 302-303. (Hall, 1988)

It also has to be noted that not every worker benefited under occupational welfare. Non-employed workers, such as farmers and the self-employed, employees of small firms with fewer than five regular workers, and non-regular employees such as part-timers and casual labourers usually insure themselves via public or other private schemes. Since the contemporary occupational welfare system had evolved in parallel with the increasing comprehensiveness of the post-war public welfare system, the relationship between occupational and state welfare schemes is worth examining. The gap in welfare benefit levels among various sized firms has been widening, especially in the areas of health-related and retirement schemes since the mid-1970s (Osawa, 1993). Osawa (1993) also argued that since the 1980s the government had focused more on the promotion and expansion of the occupational pension scheme rather than the public ones, shifting their financial burden to the market and industry. Compared with the higher growth of, for example, occupational pension plans in some larger firms, many factors including the rapidly ageing population are influencing the slow down in the development of public schemes.

Currently, of the eight public schemes, two major pension schemes cover approximately 90% of the workforce in Japan – the occupational pension scheme and the national pension scheme (Lee, 1987). The national scheme, which was established in 1961 (20 years after the establishment of the occupational scheme), covers all Japanese residents aged between 20 and 59 years old who are not covered by another public pension scheme. The two schemes differ in levels and methods of contribution. Under the occupational scheme in 1995, 17% of a worker's salary was contributed to the government, evenly split between employee and employer, while the government collects a flat contribution from members in the national scheme (¥14,000 [£70.00] per month in 1999). In the 1986 pension reform, the concept of a basic pension was introduced, and all members of the eight public pension schemes were also required to enroll in the national scheme. Since the contribution methods remain the same, retired people with an occupational scheme benefit from a basic pension from the national scheme as well as one from their occupational pension. Thus, inequalities in benefit levels between the employed workers with the occupational scheme and others with the national scheme are widening significantly (Tabata, 1990).

Overall, as a result of the 'Japanese style welfare state' having established the 'large-firm oriented' social system, those who work for small firms, day and casual labourers, female workers and those outside the labour market lose out by neither benefiting from the welfare provided by large employers nor from the state (Gould, 1993; Osawa, 1993). Consequently, a wealth gap has been created among families according to the career or employment of the principal worker of the household (Osawa, 1993). The slower economic growth in recent years, increasing global competitiveness of the economy, and people's changing attitudes to the workplace are some of the factors breaking down the nation's employment system, and thus transforming the occupational welfare system. For example, lifetime employment is no longer the principal option for Japanese workers. The loss of the 'package deal' of employment has to be substituted by other forms of welfare provision. This issue will be returned to later in this chapter.

The Role of the Family in Welfare

Based on the traditional system of 'self-help' and 'mutual aid', the high contribution of the households to welfare is another significant factor in Japan. The strain of communal solidarity or paternalistic regard for the welfare of others remains strong within households, communities, the workplace and society (Maruo, 1986). Certainly, it is the group not the individual that matters in Confucian societies; and individuals are usually deemed to be possessed of roles and duties, but not 'rights regardless' (Jones, 1993). Perhaps this cultural background is one of the reasons that Japanese society has suffered less from social anomie than other industrial nations, as reflected in Japan's low crime and divorce rates.

The family is one unit and the smallest of the whole social system. The role of the family as a welfare provider seems to be more explicitly defined in Japan, and thus the Japanese family produces more welfare, both financial and physical assistance, than families in any other industrial nation. Such practice is extended beyond the Western standard: Japanese parents usually fully support their adult children's higher education, and adult children look after their older parents(-in-law) in extended family living arrangement. In the past,[6] the family was legally obliged to provide welfare to other family members. It was not until the 1970s, at the end of a period of rapid economic growth, that Japanese social welfare legislation seemed to acknowledge the end of the family's legal obligation to provide social welfare. Despite such changes, Japanese families still feel morally obliged to provide welfare for their immediate family members.

Given the characteristics of the family role and their implicit obligations, a remarkable imbalance is found among services and benefits in the development process of the Japanese welfare state. Apart from two major public expenditures on welfare, National Health Insurance and public pension schemes, other areas of public welfare schemes such as personal social services, are considerably underdeveloped. It seems that the state's emphasis on traditional family values holds back the development of adequate public means of social service delivery and normalization schemes. The absence of public welfare provision for children, older people, or people with disabilities has had to be substituted by traditional family resources (http://www2.nttca.com:8010/infomofa/socsec/maruo/, 1 February, 1989). In contrast, some welfare programs have been established more universally. It is widely accepted, for example, that the majority of people make their children enter public school under the comprehensive education system, and go to hospitals with the National Health Insurance. Older people usually rely on the state and/or enterprises for old age pensions. Yet people still look to the informal community and the family for much personal care. Not only public appearances, but service costs and accessibility also determine the user's choice. An imbalance of the budgets, for instance, between the health insurance and social service schemes makes people depend less on costly and more accessible (non-means-tested) alternatives: older people in general tend to use medical care services and sometimes end up being *socially hospitalized* rather than choose the underdeveloped community care schemes. Overall, with changing family values and household structures, including increased numbers of nuclear family households, higher geographic mobility of younger generations, as well as the weakening of the community spirit, particularly in urban areas (Takahashi and Someya, 1985), it is increasingly difficult to keep up the traditional practices of family welfare.

Creating Social Divisions

Education and Entry to Employment

Although social policies, such as income redistribution through taxation and social transfers by the state, have contributed towards a relatively egalitarian society in Japan, the direct impact of welfare state structures on equality is becoming an issue. Indeed, the welfare state shapes class and status of citizens in a variety of ways (Esping-Andersen, 1990). In his later work, Esping-Andersen (1993) argued that the welfare state tended to dictate the choice of entry and non-entry to employment: entry into employment and subsequent job mobility can be dictated by levels of education and training programs; non-entry via the provision of a social wage option, or via its tax or service treatment of households. The education system is an obvious and frequently studied example in most post-industrial theory, affecting not only an individual's mobility chances, but also the way in which the class structures evolves (Esping-Andersen, 1990; 1993).

The Japanese education system is relatively universal but not purely state-controlled. In contemporary society, it is no longer simply part of welfare, but promotes a new class divide. The market dominates a large sphere of education available through a large private university system, and more recently, the controversial *juku* [cramming classes outside normal school hours] system. Nationally, only two in five students attend higher education such as four-year universities and two-year junior colleges, and those who graduate from the former comprise only approximately one-quarter of the relevant age group (Sugimoto, 1997). In Japan as elsewhere, educational background dictates a future career path since an increasing proportion of labour market positions are defined by educational credentials. The Japanese school system has become increasingly competitive because school and university ranks determine the point of first entry to the labour market (potential employers) and subsequent social position and wealth. For instance, Figure 4.1 indicates that the average level of the lifetime income of university graduates is twice that of those who completed only middle school education.

Figure 4.1   Disparities of age-based wages among male employees with different educational backgrounds in Japan in the early 1980s

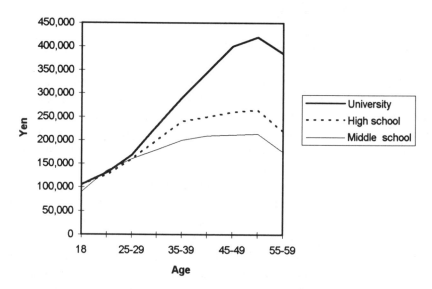

Source: Sugimoto. (1997), *An Introduction to Japanese Society*, p. 108; based on *the Basic Statistical Survey of Wage Structures* by the Ministry of Labour (1981).

Private education incurs extremely high costs in Japan so that access to such extra or prestigious education is strongly tied into accumulated family wealth. Providing high quality education to a younger generation usually reinforces family wealth, which promises to provide high quality education again to the next generation. Table 4.3 shows that the chances of getting into national universities did not purely depend on family wealth, compared to access to private universities, where parental incomes would seem to have been a major factor (Gould, 1993). The exception is, however, found in the top national university where a majority of the students have higher income family background in relation to their financial ability to support long preparation periods of prestigious education prior to entry.

Table 4.3 Percentage distribution of university students by family income and type of university in Japan (1974)

	Lowest quintile	2	3	4	Highest quintile
National universities	14.4	11.2	16.0	24.3	34.1
Private universities	6.1	6.5	11.6	21.2	54.6

Source: Gould. (1993), *Capitalist Welfare Systems*, p. 61.

The Woman's Position in the Family, the Labour Market and Society

The welfare state has created not only class stratification through education but also division of labour by gender (Langan and Ostner, 1991; Yasukochi, 1995; Yazawa, 1993). In Japan, the post-war development of the social system, based on the patriarchal gender relationship (Osawa, 1993), contributed to the creation of new gender inequalities in the family and society. The male breadwinner family model, which has been modified in modern welfare states such as Japan, operated most fully for late-nineteenth century middle class families in industrial societies such as Britain and Ireland (Lewis, 1992). Within a 'male-dominated' social system, the social security system in Japan has been developed based on the 'family as a unit' instead of on an individual basis. It reinforced gender roles in the family such as the male as the breadwinner and the female as the unpaid domestic or care worker in order to enhance available resources within the family (Takenaka, 1996). The woman's role in the family was then defined as providing their spouse with basic living security by means of forming a household (Osawa, 1993). Japanese women, therefore, had typically gained welfare entitlement not by their own right and qualification, but by virtue of their dependent status within the family as wives and mothers. Such a mechanism prevented women from becoming economically independent, and also generated an economic 'bond' between couples. Under 'the family as a unit' system, women alone could not gain access to, and status in, paid employment, social security rights and benefits as equally as men. Women had thus tended to make contributions and draw benefits via their husband on the basis of an assumed male breadwinner family model. Within such a 'male-dominated' and 'the family as a unit' society, women outside a conventional family structure are particularly disadvantaged. Since divorce has not been considered a part of a normatively defined 'proper' life-course in Japanese society, the deterioration of the family unit by divorce or early widowhood often leads women into a particularly disadvantaged position (Meguro, 1987). Because of gender differences in levels of and access to income and welfare benefits, poverty is often found in female-headed households (Meguro, 1987).

Even though more than half of all women in the working population[7] are currently engaged in waged labour, women, especially married women, are often discriminated against and discouraged from equal employment opportunities and income in Japan (Yoshida, 1993). By excluding married women from the regular labour market, Japan has succeeded in maintaining full-employment – the unemployment rates had been less than 3% until the prolonged post-bubble recession increased the rate to around 3.5% in 1997 (http://www2.nttca.com:8010/infomofa/socsec/maruo, 1 February 1998), and reached a record 4.3% in June 1998 (*Asahi Evening News*, 31 July 1998). Even after the Equal Employment Opportunity Act in 1986, gender discrimination in salary, promotion, hiring processes and other workplace-related issues remains. A married woman who is unemployed is often better off on average than her counterpart who has a career. The current taxation and pension policies of the government have been crucial preconditions for women's absence from the labour market. The system of discriminatory tax treatment of two income households discourages wives from taking a full-time job which pays more than ¥1,300,000 (£6,500) annually. Many married women try not to exceed the maximum earning limit and to stay in a dependent status in order to benefit fully from the taxation and welfare system, and maintain maximum income of the two earners (*Asahi Shinbun*, 24 August 1995, p.19). In fact, according to a survey conducted by the Ministry of Labour in 1986, among employees in the *paat* [part-time] status[8], 700,000 out of 1,200,000 were women and the majority were assumed to be married. As a result, instead of promoting gender equalities in the labour market, an expansion of female workers since the Equal Opportunity Act has been concentrated on fringe work such as part-time jobs (Osawa, 1993). The contemporary pension system in the mid-1980s was also developed and reinforced to protect housewives rather than working women. For instance, widows who have never worked are often able to receive more pension (their husband's bereaved pension) than their counterparts who had a career, which often makes married women lose the incentive to take up a full-time job (*Asahi Shinbun*, 26 August 1995, p.17). In addition, under the current system, formerly-employed widows are entitled to receive only one pension, either their own or their spouse's bereaved pension. Reflecting differences in their salaries, the majority tend to choose their spouse's pension and to give up their own despite the contributions paid throughout the years employed. The fragmented pension system has started posing a question of such inequalities in contribution and benefit levels among women according to their marital and employment status (Takahashi and Someya, 1985; *Asahi Shinbun*, 19 April 1998, p.4).

Furthermore, married women can be disadvantaged due to inbuilt institutional constraints, ranging from the absence of collective social services including child and old age care to maternity rights. Those factors often put them into the position of having to choose either paid work or having a child. So far, social and employment structures are not established enough to allow women to become working mothers. Traditionally, the low participation of males in domestic work also leaves working wives and mothers with a heavy burden of incompatible duties. For these women, frustration and feelings of guilt about the family are amplified (Yasukochi, 1995). The characteristics of women's labour force participation is generally characterized as 'M-shape employment' (Figure 4.2).

The drop from the first peak is caused by marriage and childbirth and the drop from the second peak can be considered to be due to the necessity of old age care for their parents(-in-law). Thus, the traditional *Ie* [the family] norm has been another factor consolidating the contemporary labour market and welfare policies. All these factors have resulted in women postponing marriage and child-bearing in recent years, and has led to a marked decrease in birth-rates. The concept of 'DINKS (double income no kids)' became popular in the late 1980s in order to achieve a high (or decent) living standard by two earners. Even after the introduction of maternity leave with income compensation for female employees of the

1990s, birth-rates have not increased substantially. This can be related to the low benefit levels or more socially constructed reasons: maternity benefit is still as low as 20% of wages from employment insurance funds and social insurance contribution from employers; and social pressure in the workplace may discourage women from taking maternity leave and instead, they may simply leave the firm. Such low birth-rates have accentuated the process of an ageing Japanese population, a process which will eventually require more public expenditure on welfare and raise the social service demands of older people.

Figure 4.2 International comparison of female labour participation rates (%)

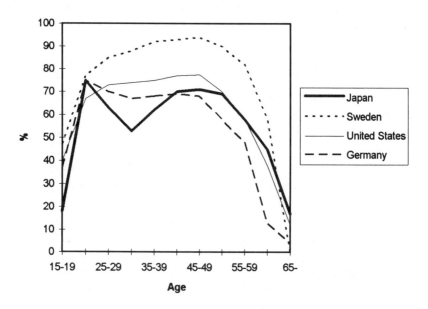

Source: Sugimoto. (1997), *An Introduction to Japanese Society*, p. 144. (adapted from *Forum 1994*, p.33 [based on ILO's *Year Book of Labour Statistics*. The German data are taken from West German statistics before unification]).

Minority Groups in Japan

Minority and ethnicity issues have received little attention in Japanese social research, compared with other multi-racial and multi-ethnic societies.

Japan's characteristically homogeneous population is partly due to the pre-war history of *sakoku* [the isolation policy of the *Edo* period][9] and more recent restrictive immigration policies represented by the Immigration Control Law of 1990.[10] As a result, inequality in social status, employment opportunities, or access to the welfare benefits exists between the majority of Japanese and minority groups in Japan. The members of minority groups (comprising approximately 4% of the 125 million people in Japan) are likely to be of Japanese origin (e.g. *burakumin* [descendants of a historical outcast group], of foreign origin (e.g. permanent residents from Korea and China who were brought to Japan as colonial labour during the Wars, and their second and third generations), or different races living in Japan (e.g. the *Ainu* race [the indigenous population of northern Japan]) (Sugimoto, 1997). Immigrant workers, often illegal, from overseas, are also a new minority group in the 1990s.

Unlike other industrial societies, Japan managed to achieve high levels of economic growth without relying on foreign manual workers until the early 1980s. During the bubble-economy period of the late 1980s, however, Japan experienced an economic upswing followed by a severe shortage of labour, which generated a massive inflow of illegal foreign workers, predominantly male, into Japan (Sellek, 1997). The shortage of labour was particularly serious in labour-intensive industries such as manufacturing, construction and the service sector. These jobs have been shunned by younger Japanese workers not only due to the nature of the work being '3K' ('3D' in English) (*kitsui, kitanai,* and *kiken* [difficult, dirty, and dangerous]), but also due to the poor working conditions and low wages (Mori, 1995; Sellek and Weiner, 1992). In response to the labour shortage in the unskilled job sector, Japan decided to partially open its doors to desirable workers.

Under the current Immigration Control Law, only *nikkeijin* [mainly South American-Japanese descendants up to the third generation and their spouses] are allowed to work legally in the unskilled job sector.[11] However, the policy inviting *nikkeijin* to fill the unskilled job sector has not stopped the illegal migration of manual workers from overseas. In recent years, therefore, governments have started addressing the problems of how to incorporate those new immigrant workers into society. Many issues including the provision of compensation for industrial accidents, medical care and welfare, Japanese language course, and housing remain unresolved for the *nikkeijin* workers and their families, let alone other illegal workers (Sellek, 1997). Educational provision for *nikkeijin* children (as permanent settlers) has also become a critical issue since their language incapability is likely to drive them out of school and thus restrict employment opportunities open to them. This may, in turn, raise social costs due to increased welfare provision and a higher incidence of crime.

The minority populations in general have experienced disadvantage and discrimination in many areas of socio-economic and legal systems. For example, discrimination against second and third generation Koreans and Chinese (who were born and brought up in Japan, and who often only speak Japanese) is still significant in areas such as job recruitment, promotion, eligibility for welfare benefits, holding public office and other civil rights (Sugimoto, 1997). Discrimination against the minority groups in the housing sector is also widespread. Some property owners and estate agents explicitly require tenants to be Japanese nationals (Sugimoto, 1997). In the context of welfare provision, these Koreans or other permanent residents were not entitled to join the National Pension Plan until 1982. Also, new immigrant workers due to their subordinate position in the labour market do not benefit equally in terms of income or general welfare in the same way as full-time Japanese workers (Sellek, 1997). For members of minority groups, therefore, acquiring the right to full citizenship or equality remains difficult. Arguably, the lack of considerations for minority issues has relegated the subject in policy debate. Indeed, an increasing number of governments are currently working to achieve more integration: by developing effective social and educational programs for new return-migrants; and by removing the nationality requirement for public office or teaching positions (Sellek, 1997; Sugimoto, 1997).

Post-Bubble Welfare State: Issues and Direction

An increasing proportion of older people in the total population over the next century will increase the total volume of required welfare such as social security expenditure and social services. In response, the Japanese welfare state is continuously transforming into the post-bubble economy phase of the twenty-first century within the increasingly limited resources. The major concern and debates in this scenario are around the balance between the working population and the dependant population in an ageing society. Since social security expenditure is usually considered a burden in terms of economic efficiency and economic growth, the government started to cut back public expenditure on welfare in the late 1990s. Consequently, the qualifying age for public pensions has been raised so that every citizen, including students over 20 years old, has to make contributions. Patient fees and extra charges for drugs were added to National Health Insurance coverage for older people. So far, the public seem to have accepted those backward changes without much resistance, partly due to the government's success at raising public awareness regarding the ageing society, and the potential costs this will entail.

One argument, however, stresses that older people and people currently outside the labour market are not necessarily all dependant. Many of these people, especially the growing number of healthy old people (young-olds), could be considered not as a residual section of society, but as a potential labour force under the concept of *productive ageing* (http://www2. nttca.com:8010/infomofa/socsec/maruo/, 1 February 1998). On the supply side of economy, the encouragement of employment for such a potentially 'dependant population' will contribute to raising GDP and tax revenue, and save on social security expenditure. Not only paid work, but the voluntary participation of older people in welfare service delivery could benefit both the government, by reducing the burden of social security, and older people by raising their *ikigai* [meaning of life] in old age. Such reorganization of available human resources could also serve as one of the solutions to substituting the decreasing family function for conventional old age care. Since Japan's labour-short economy can be explained partly as a consequence of married women's lack of labour force participation, these housewives could have the assets and time necessary to involve themselves in managing and delivering social services. In this scenario, women's experiences in family support could be useful in caring for strangers, which is not likely to involve the same level of emotional strain as caring for their own parents(-in-law). It will again contribute to increasing GDP. However, this strategy is also likely to create and reinforce a new division of labour by gender in the social service sector.

The second argument is that in the post-bubble period over the twenty-first century, the welfare state is becoming more market-oriented and organized along a contract basis. In a sense, it is moving closer to the American model of a 'liberal-residual' welfare state. In other words, welfare services will not be granted freely and universally from the state, the traditional family, or enterprises, but will increasingly become based on a contract between users and various welfare providers. The prolonged post-bubble recession, the continuing high appreciation of the yen, the increasing global competitiveness of the market, and the rapidly ageing working population – all these economic-related factors are influencing the break-down of the conventional employment system and have forced a review of such 'Japanese-style management' (e.g. hiring practices and salary structures) (Miyajima, 1997; http://www.jinjapan.org/insight/html/, 28 May 1998).

One example is the disappearing package deal of the conventional occupational benefits, which was once a symbol of the post-war employment system in Japan.   Matsushita Electronic (National), once a famous representative of 'the firm as the family' model, has recently introduced *post-shuushin-koyou* [post-lifetime employment system] (*Asahi Shinbun*, 5 January 1998, p.1).   According to the new system which Matsushita selectively introduced to 800 new recruits in 1997, instead of providing voluntary occupational benefits such as retirement allowance and low interest (housing) loans and saving schemes, the firm were willing to pay more cash wages annually during the employees' years with the firm.   Some other large firms including Kaoh, Recruit and Sanwa Research Institute also followed this new post-bubble employment trend.   In the late 1990s, as a consequence, only 16.5% of Japanese workers are employed by well-established companies or the public sector, and enjoy security of employment with full benefits, compared to approximately one-third during the high growth period between the 1960s and the early 1970s (http://www.jinjapan.org/insight/html/, 28 May 1998).   Additionally, in order to cut costs and achieve greater productivity, many firms have started replacing those workers on full benefits with more flexible workers to meet their changing needs.   The breakdown of the conventional system indicates that individuals are forced to become more independent from their firm and take more responsibility to plan their own life-course.   This fact symbolizes changing patterns in the labour market, from the family orientation of the workplace to a more flexible, competitive, individualistic and meritocratic type of employment system.   However, market-oriented policies may increase inequality in income and assets and create a new social division.

Following this trend, the relationship between the state and individuals is also becoming organized more along a contract basis. Legislation recently passed for the 'public insurance of nursing care' is a good example.   The system has emerged from an awareness of the increasing ageing population and the decreasing capacity of conventional family support, while the limited public resources are becoming more difficult to match older people's needs.   The new system would make it clear to the public that old age care is no longer granted either by the traditional family or the state, but has become based on an individual's contribution. Many issues, however, remain uncertain for the successful implementation of the system. A common criticism is to doubt whether so many home helps, both qualified and unqualified, can be found in Japan's labour-short economy. Also, issues such as how to improve the current unfavourable working condition of home helps, and how to improve fairness in the assessment procedure to be qualified for services are still in question (Ueno in *Asahi Shinbun*, 22 December 1997, p. 4). Overall, this shift can be seen as one step forward to form a new relationship between service users and providers, the household and women, in the post-bubble welfare state.

Furthermore, the current social security rights and contributions based on 'a family unit' need to be reviewed to take account of more individualistic arrangements in order to promote equalities among people of different marital status and of family structure. An individual-based social security system will eventually promote each person's independence and social rights, and reduce gender roles between couples in the family (between paid and unpaid work) (Takenaka, 1996). In order to establish gender equality in social security systems, such equality has to be achieved in employment since women's low social security benefits reflects their low salary and unpaid work. Both revised labour and social policies are needed to strengthen women's economic independence.

Concluding Comments

This chapter has outlined the origin, structure and transformation of the post-war welfare state in Japan. In the process of the shift from feudalism to a capitalist state during the first half of the twentieth century, Japanese economic development was influenced by Western industrial societies, and the institutional framework of the welfare state also originated in mature European models. As for the contemporary state, through the reconstruction period after the Second World War, the US influence on Japan's post-war economic and institutional re-establishment was inevitable. Given these facts, it is not surprising that the welfare state in Japan has evolved by adapting various elements of existing Western welfare regimes – indeed, the Japanese welfare state is often described as a combination of the 'liberal-residual' and 'conservative-corporatist' model. Furthermore, since Japan's cultural characteristics such as the Confucian practice of the family, community and workplace have survived through the years, these have added a different flavour to the conventional Western models. Sustaining the strong informal sector, Japan had developed a residual welfare state with a large role played by the market and enterprises by the 1990s.

Since the welfare state in Japan, as in most other societies, is still in the process of transition, a shift in the balance among various sectors and relationships between users and providers within *the mixed economy of welfare* is currently taking place. The next chapter explores how older women are coping with the current shift away from traditional family reliance. As we approach the twenty-first century, the Japanese welfare state in the post-bubble era is, indeed, facing an inevitable turning point. Considering the prolonged post-bubble recession and rapid societal ageing, the Japanese residual welfare approach will come under strain since welfare provision by both the family and enterprises are threatened.

In such present and future conditions, many aspects of conventional post-war welfare provision such as social security and personal old age care will become more market-oriented and more likely to be organized on a contract basis. For example, there are already many indicators that the post-war employment system which provided employees with extensive occupational welfare will be difficult to maintain. Instead, the employment pattern will become more flexible, resulting in the majority of workers being required to insure themselves in the market. Other evidence of the transformation is found in the informal sector. Declining capacity and willingness of the family to take part in welfare provision will require an alternative means to family support.

The post-war welfare state enforced gender roles in the family to sustain unpaid female domestic workers, and thus placed women in a disadvantaged position. More recently, women have resisted these practices by entering higher education and the labour market in increasing numbers, through the postponement of marriage and child-bearing, which has started putting pressure on existing systems. For the welfare state of the twenty-first century to achieve more equalities among families and individuals and between genders, the nature of Japanese society – presently 'male-dominated,' with an employment system predominantly 'large-firm oriented', and with social security systems based on 'the family as a unit' – will all be put under great pressure. Indeed, the next chapter presents a further analysis as to how the social system and labour market mechanism have determined women's status (especially, their economic status) in society. It also identifies which group of women were particularly disadvantaged and investigates the reasons for the outcome.

Notes

1   Average annual real GDP growth rates per capita during 1870-1938, 1950-73, and 1973-87 were: 1.81%, 8.15% and 2.83% respectively.

2   The definition of social security sometimes includes not only income security but also health service benefits and personal social service benefits. Social security benefits mean social security payments both in cash and in kind.

3   '*Akahige*' is also a title of a novel written by Yamamoto Shugorou in 1958.

4   'Administrative guidance' is a method, rather than a policy, widely used by the Japanese government to support or reinforce many sorts of policies, both micro-economic and macro-economic. Essentially, it involves the use of influence, advice and persuasion to cause firms or individuals to behave in particular ways that the government believes are desirable. The persuasion of course is exerted and the advice given by public officials who may have the power to provide, or withhold, loans, grants, subsidies, licenses, tax concessions, government contracts, permission to import, foreign exchange, approval of cartel arrangements and other desirable outcomes. The Japanese tradition of private acceptance of government leadership and the widespread recognition that government officials have knowledge, experience and information superior to that available to the ordinary firm, as well as the sharing of values, beliefs and political preferences by government officials and business leaders, all contribute to the success of the method (Tsuru, 1993).

5   6 *tatami*-mat is equivalent to 9.72 m^2.

6   The revised National Assistance Act in 1950 stated that public assistance was supplementary to assistance offered by relatives, who should be primary supporters.

7   The working population is usually defined as people between 15 and 65 years of age. In 1991, women's labour force participation reached 50.7%, and they were concentrated in the tertiary industry (Sugimoto, 1997).

8   The definition of 'part-time' employment varies among countries. In Japan, *paat* [part-timer] covers not only those employees with limited working hours, but also those who work as long as full-time workers but who are employed on a fixed-term basis and in hourly-wage based without fringe and occupational based social security benefits.

9   Japan closed its country for two centuries during the *Edo* period (1603-1867), leaving only two commercial links with China and Holland. With the increasing contact with European traders and missionaries in the early seventeenth century, the Tokugawa government felt that the foreign influences, particularly Christianity, were a threat to the stability of the country. Many Japanese who left and returned during this period were executed to prevent the introduction of outside ideas. The isolation was brought to an end with the arrival of the Black Ships of Commodore Perry (US) in 1853 with a demand that Japan open its doors to trade.

10   The Immigration Control and Refugee Recognition Act (1990) in Japan states that the government will only accept foreigners who possess some special skill not held by Japanese nationals.

11   The privileged position of nikkeijin has been criticized since discrimination in employment based on race or ethnicity (with its emphasis on blood lineage) is increasingly at odds with trends in other industrial nations, and also in Brazil (Sellek, 1997).

5   Women and the Welfare State

Introduction

Through the development of post-war employment and welfare structures, the idea of the 'family as a unit' has emerged. Accordingly, these systems created and reinforced women's dependency upon their spouses and society. As elaborated in the previous chapter, it was inevitable that systems based on the male breadwinner family model had socially and often institutionally constructed gender roles – indeed, the role of women in society was clearly defined and embedded in many Japanese families. For example, despite the worldwide feminist movement of the 1960s and 1970s, a gender-segregated curriculum was applied in Japanese schools until the late 1980s. In junior high and high schools (age 13 to 18-years-old), it was common for only girls to take 'home economics' classes to learn how to cook and sew, while boys took traditional Japanese martial arts (e.g. *Judo* and *Kendo*) or carpentry classes. Indeed, at the workplace, female workers are still expected to clean their offices every morning, and to serve tea to their male colleagues, except in the most progressive of companies.

One of the objectives in this chapter is to illustrate the roles and positions of women in the family and society through the experiences of the older women who were interviewed. This is followed by an analysis of how their roles and status have been transformed in recent years. By interviewing women of different socio-economic status, this chapter also aims to investigate the causes and processes whereby such systems help to create inequalities or wealth gaps among women in old age.

Traditionally, women's duties included caring for other family members. The second part of this chapter, therefore, highlights and examines these issues in the context of decreasing family traditions and the newly forming welfare systems. If the family is no longer a viable and reliable option for care in old age, a shift to alternative sources of support, both via the state and in the market, will inevitably occur. How older people's deeply embedded cultural identity copes with these changes is also of interest, and the chapter explores how the current transformation of the welfare system is affecting older women's views and attitudes generally.

Women's Position in the Family and Society

Women in the Male Breadwinner Family Model

In Japan, marriage usually defined women's position and status in society. By acquiring a husband, children, and parents-in-law through marriage, women were acknowledged in society, and given certain tasks and obligations to perform in the family – mostly domestic duties and care work. The gender roles of the married couples – husbands acting as breadwinners and wives as domestic and care workers – were rather explicitly defined and carried out in Japanese families, which usually resulted in them not being involved in their opposite gender's tasks. Consequently, women were often excluded from, or disadvantaged by, the formal labour market, and their husbands remained unwilling or sometimes incapable of doing 'female' domestic work:

> A.A (72) *"In the past, it used to be said that 'men were not allowed to enter the kitchen'. Accordingly, my husband was not even able to boil water. So, whenever I had to go out, it was a big hassle for me – I had to get everything ready for him at home, including leaving hot water in a thermos bottle. He was not an exception, though. That's why, when husbands like him without domestic skills are left alone [become a widower], it is so miserable and pathetic not being able to take care of themselves that they have to move into their adult children's house, residential homes, or nursing homes."*

Another key reason for women staying at home to carry out domestic duties was the labour market mechanism created through post-war industrialization. In the process of the transformation from an agricultural to an industrial society, the majority of Japanese workers, mainly males, had become employed in either secondary or tertiary industries. The older women continued to accept their domestic role, labouring without direct cash rewards and following widely held conventional norms. As a result, the post-war employment structure further consolidated gender roles in the family. The position of the husband as a sole wage earner was further reinforced:

> O.K (77) had been a housewife, having carried out all domestic work, child care for her grandson, and old age care for her bed-ridden husband for six years. *"I think that [such gender roles] are a lot to do with post-war social and economic change. Maybe, the family has become more individualistic. In agricultural society, it was not a problem since all family members had a task, and jobs were distributed equally among them. But, it's a different scenario if your husband is a 'salary-man' [employed]."*

> K.H (73) worked as a casual labourer to earn 'pocket money' in between her domestic duties. *"My husband was a very strict man. He didn't like me going out without good cause. If I did, he was very hysterical, accusing me of hanging around outside the house. That's why, even working for six days a month, it became a very good reason to go out from the house and make little pocket money that I could spend for myself."*

Caring for family members was usually expected to be a women's duty in the male breadwinner family model. Regardless of blood or in-law relations, it was evident that care in old age was unreservedly left with women in the family. This made it very difficult, if not impossible, for married women to have a dual commitment to care work and a full-time paid job. That was one of the reasons why those women often remained as secondary wage earners in the households, working part-time or even more casually in order to secure time for such domestic duties. In contrast, male members of the family, who were supposed to be engaged with full-time paid work, were usually absent from (and frequently not even expected to do) domestic work:

> Even while N.H (70) was working full-time in a local authority office, caring for her coresident mother-in-law was her duty rather than her spouse's. She had been bed-ridden for 15 years. *"Since my office was within walking distance from my home, I used to dash back home every lunch time in order to feed my mother-in-law and change her nappies. Her own daughter usually came in the afternoon to look after her."*

> O.M (78) lived with her eldest son and his family in their own home. *"Five of us, women, made a rota to look after my bed-ridden husband.*

Even when he was in hospital, it was a heavy burden to look after him in the morning, in the afternoon, and over night. All the women in the family, my two daughters and two daughters-in-law, helped out. If I had been on my own, I, myself, would have become ill. My coresident son's wife was a full-time nursery teacher before. She had a good job which was going very well. So, it was a bit of a shame that she had to quit the job to take care of my husband."

O.T (71) lived with her unmarried eldest daughter (46). After her spouse's early death, her eldest daughter got a job in a bank, and supported her family financially. She paid her younger brother's higher education fees. *"If I become bed-ridden, I can't ask my daughter to quit her job and look after me. She is single, and working like a man [being a breadwinner]. It's the same thing that you would never ask your son to quit his job in order to give you personal care."*

The employment mechanism usually placed further restrictions upon married women entering the formal labour market. Despite their wishes, many women faced obstacles when trying to develop their own careers. Unless they had professional jobs, such as teachers, nurses, or civil servants, single women tended not to be able to gain economic independence in the family and society. Because such a family model created and reinforced gender roles in households, as well as gender inequalities in employment opportunities and income, 'marriage' used to be the dominant option for women to survive and secure their financial position in society. Indeed, it seemed to explain why the nation experienced 'full marriage' rates in the post-war industrialization periods. In other words, such a family system inevitably marginalized the position and economic status of women, who were single by divorce, widowhood, or had never been married.

In recent years, gradually but inexorably, changes in the family system have been occurring. Both women's increasing rates of labour market participation and decreasing interests and unwillingness to adapt conventional roles in marriage are putting the existing employment and welfare systems under great pressure. With growing numbers of women entering the labour market on a more regular basis, increasing numbers of women are likely to become economically independent both inside and outside of marriage. Despite the gender inequalities in the labour market, the options of Japanese women have expanded:

O.K (77)'s daughter died of cancer at 42. After her death, her daughter's spouse remained a coresident with O.K and her spouse in their own single-family home. *"I think that women these days are much more independent. After my daughter died, it was very difficult for her widowed husband [my son-in-law] to find a woman to remarry. We could not find anyone. Suitable and eligible women in his age usually had their own income sufficient to support themselves. Even for a young bachelor these days, if he doesn't receive adequate income or isn't attractive enough, no girl wants to marry him, let alone, a middle-aged widower like my son-in-law who earns only a small salary! If women don't need to depend on a man's financial ability, who wants to marry and look after a husband and his parents-in-law at home!"*

Women in the Labour Market

Gender roles and inequalities were not only evident in the conventional family model, but expanded into the labour market itself. In general, the post-war employment system in Japan, which was strongly male-dominated, often excluded women from the formal labour market. Women were simply not given equal access to or equivalent status in the formal labour market compared to men. Indeed, women's employment opportunities were limited, and they were often disadvantaged at the workplace:

S.Y (74) left her spouse at 20, six months after their marriage. She had worked throughout her adult life to support herself financially. For the last 30 years until her retirement, she had worked as a shop clerk in a big department store. She lived in rental housing provided by *Juutaku Toshi Seibi Koudan* [the Housing Corporation].[1] *"Since I wasn't good at flattering my male boss, I had not received much in the way of pay rises. Also, because I was a woman, my salary and retirement allowance were very low. As a single woman, my salary was nothing to compare with my male counterparts 'who were supporting their dependent family'. In my workplace, there was no concept of fairness in pay awards or equality in income or treatment among employees, especially between genders. When I complained about an unfair pay raise to the personnel department, I was just told that it was my own fault."*

The research illustrated that older women currently in poverty, living in state sector housing, were more likely to have worked to make ends meet than other female groups who were likely to be supported by their spouse. As a result of the male-dominated employment system, however, many of those women who had worked for a living were engaged in the informal sector of employment, for example, helping out in their family business. They may also have had an irregular or unstable work status (e.g. *paat* [working the same hours as full-time employees, but in a temporary status without social security benefits and contributions]). Marriage breakdown either by divorce or early widowhood, which meant losing the principal male worker of the household, was the main reason why women were placed in such an unfavourable economic situation. Consequently, these women were forced to enter the labour market without many work skills and experiences in their middle age:

> K.H (79) lived in a publicly-funded home for older people without any pension or savings. Her spouse had been bed-ridden for 10 years in their 40s while their six children were still growing up. *"Because I had to care for my sick husband, I couldn't take up a formal, full-time job. That's why I worked as 'paat' which allowed me more flexibility to look after my husband.... But, instead, in order to make up the time and earn more money, I did lots of overtime in the evening."*

> A.A (74) divorced her *youshi* spouse a year after their marriage. After her divorce, she had worked as a housemaid for various families, and then as a domestic kitchen and cleaning worker in a private clinic. She moved into a home for older people when she was 71. *"For women like me who had only graduated from a 'former higher-elementary school'[2], work opportunities had been very slim. Places where women alone [not as a couple doing family business] could work were very limited – usually bars or nightclubs, and a housemaid at best."*

> N.M (75) moved into a public home for older people when she was 67. *"I had been helping out in my husband's barber shop until I divorced him at 57. Then, I started working as 'paat' in a restaurant kitchen. After five years, I fell down the stairs in my rented apartment and stayed in hospital with a broken hip. I lost income because I couldn't work after the accident. So, I went to a welfare office and asked if I could get public assistance for living protection."*

> O.T (71)'s spouse died when she was 42. After his death, she had a house built on the land which her spouse left. *"When my husband passed away, I had to start working. My three children were still in school age. You know, while my husband was alive, I had never worked – I had never done anything outside the house. Since my husband died*

at 39, we couldn't live on my small widow's pension. Do you think that I could get an office job at 40? No way! [The only job which middle-aged women could get was] in the service trade. A waitress in a Japanese restaurant. I used to get dinner ready for my children before going out to work in the evening. I had worked there for 13 years until my eldest daughter graduated from high school and started supporting the family."

Women and Social Security

The post-war development of the social security system was another reason which encouraged women to marry, and further reinforced gender roles and economic relationships among married couples. Through marriage, women acquired the position and status of *shufu* [a housewife]. These housewives were usually granted access to social security, health services, and social position through their spouse's employed status and welfare contributions. The system, which had been developed based on 'the family as a unit', was intended to provide married women with social and financial protection without the need for them to take up full-time employment. From another perspective, the system tied these women to their home and discouraged them from seeking formal employment. Among all the social security programs, the national pension scheme provides a good example. The pension reform introduced in 1986 dramatically strengthened the position of housewives.

Under the new system, if their spouse is employed and has an occupational pension scheme, his contributions automatically cover those of his wife for the basic national pension scheme without any extra contributions. This privileged status of housewives is highlighted by the fact that single males have to make the same amount of contributions as their married counterparts if they earn the same incomes. In contrast, women without a legal male partner have not always been afforded the same privileges:

T.S (76) had been a housewife, having domestically supported her spouse who was a teacher. After her spouse's death, she bought a life-estate in a private purpose-built retirement flat. *"My widow's pension is sufficient for me to live comfortably on my own. I didn't even need to sell our own house in order to move into this flat."*

A.Y (71) had never been married, although she had always been with her older sister. Like a married couple, she had helped her sister's business, working in her beauty saloon. Later on when her sister got divorced and started a cafe in a different city, she also moved with her sister, continuing to work for her in the cafe. After her sister died, she moved into a public home for older people. Even though she was like a partner to her sister, her position and financial status were not at all protected like a housewife. *"I am in limbo at present – my basic national pension [around ¥70,000 (£350) a month] is too small to live on without any income support. But, since I receive the pension, I'm not poor enough to be fully subsidized by the state. I have little savings and no property. I had always depended on my sister until she died last year. Although I had fulfilled my role helping her business, I wasn't insured as a formal employee. Unlike wives who had supported their husband in the family, I can't receive a widow's pension after my sister's death, either."*

On the other hand, the system did not favour married women in career positions. Due to the social security system being based upon 'the family as a unit', these 'career widows' were able to receive only one occupational-based pension, either their own or their bereaved spouse's pension (approximately 75% of the occupational component of pensions). Despite making their own contributions throughout their working lives, many career women were likely to give up their own pension after their spouse's death. This indicates that the life-income of career women was usually less than a male worker's partial income. It is understandable, therefore, that single career women were resistant to this system. Their own and only pension which they had contributed to by themselves was very likely to be less than that of widows who had never worked:

U.Y (70) had worked as a nursery teacher until her retirement. Her spouse was a public servant. She lived in an owned single-family home. *"I had worked as a nursery teacher for 20 years, and then as a chief of a nursery school for another 20 years. As a nursery teacher, I worked for a small school run by a temple. It wasn't an established institution so that my status was informal. Those 13 years working for the particular school made a big empty hole in my contribution years to the occupational pension plan. That's why I am not eligible to receive my own occupational pension.... You know, my contribution years didn't reach all the required periods of 25 or 35 years. It is now too late to go back and make up the absent years, anyway. When my husband passed away, I chose to receive my widow's pension, which was only half of what we used to receive together, but still much more than my own."*

N.H (79) had worked for 30 years in the local authority office until her retirement at 60. At the time of interview, she lived with her son and his family in a newly-built single-family home. *"It must be a rare case that I have been receiving my own occupational pension after my husband's death. Mine was better than his 75%. I worked as a public servant [which is as gender equal as you can get in the Japanese labour market], while my husband had worked for a small private company."*

Some occupational welfare schemes were more established and provided a higher degree of benefit than the basic national ones. Regardless of gender, informal labourers were, therefore, disadvantaged both in terms of their basic remuneration and the levels of benefits which they could receive. Single women especially without a male principal worker in their households were likely to be placed in such a disadvantaged situation. These people had typically lived a day-to-day life without any concerns for the future or foresight to plan for their financial security in old age. In terms of pensions, working as *paat* throughout their life, those people did not have access to the occupational pension scheme. Consequently, the research found greater poverty among single older women who had not had a stable male partner to support them financially, and thus who worked informally and who were left without any pension in their old age:

K.H (79) had worked as *paat* while she was looking after her sick spouse. She had no pension, and thus her occupancy charge to live in a public home was minimal. *"After my husband got sick and gave up work, I worked very hard instead of him. At that time, there was no occupational pension scheme in my workplace. Since I was working as 'paat', I was not insured by the company, anyway. I couldn't contribute to any pension plan, including the basic national scheme. If I had paid for pension contributions, we, our family, would not have been able to eat. I had no spare money to contribute towards a pension plan, let alone set aside money for the future."*

Y.M (76) rented an old wooden house, subsidized fully by the local authority. She and her spouse sold their house in Saga (the neighbouring prefecture), and moved to the city with funds from selling their house. *"We had enough money to be picky about jobs when we first moved to the city. If we didn't like the job, we quit and found another one. We worked as a warden of a company dormitory and in a multi-storey flat, and also worked for places like a public bath. While the money lasted, we were able to do so. Perhaps, that's the reason why we didn't stay in any one job for long. Within two years, we had moved around eight times. Well, by the time my husband got ill, we had exhausted all our money and had no occupational-related insurance. Although it became my responsibility to earn some money for living, such a stressful situation also made me sick. When both of us were hospitalized, we had no choice but to go on welfare [public assistance for living protection]."*

A.A (74) moved into a public home for older people at 71. She also divorced her *youshi* spouse one year after their marriage. Leaving her only daughter with her mother, she worked informally as a live-in housemaid for different families. *"I always found something which I did not like about the family, and quit working for them. I repeatedly did so. So, I didn't work for any one of the families for more than three years.... At that time, being on my own, I knew little of the world. So, I had no clue, or never thought about securing my future welfare. Luckily enough, someone told me before it was too late, and I went back and contributed as much as I could to make up for those absent years. Thank God, now, even a little occupational pension, I can receive it! If only I had known about it before, I would have chosen workplaces which offered occupational welfare. If so, my life could have been much easier. I did not have a sense of personal finance."*

In contrast, women with formal employment status often led better lives later on with their own pension. Apart from being a professional, working in the family business could be another possibility for women in the research cohort to gain economic independence from their spouse in old age. In the case of a family business, not remaining self-employed (without occupational-based social security), but establishing a small company employing more than five workers on a formal basis (with occupational welfare) appeared to be the initial step to bring security to the family as well as to other employees. It also made a noticeable difference to women's economic independence in old age whether wives had been employed formally within the established system or had remained as informal labourers. The research highlighted that among women who had worked on a regular basis, those widows who engaged in a family business on a formal or employed status were more likely to be better-off and economically independent with their own pension. Gender roles were less emphasized in such 'self-employed' families, compared to the 'salaried' ones. In addition, the status of these women was less dependent on their spouse financially, compared with housewives:

> N.T (74) lived with her eldest son and his family in her own single-family home. After her spouse's death, her son took over his family plumbing business. *"Indeed, self-employed [family] business needs both of our [husband and wife's] hands. It won't work if a wife doesn't know the details [of the business]. Now, my daughter-in-law is helping my son as I helped my husband for over 30 years. When my husband first started the company, he also employed me as an office clerk with occupational benefits. We used to contribute to the national pension scheme before we started the business. But, at that time, I had no idea how important it was [to join the occupational schemes] in order to receive my own pension later on. I had never thought about the pension system or its mechanism. After my husband died, his pension was cut off, and I'm currently receiving only my own pension. It is enough to live on. Now, I'm glad that I contributed to the occupational scheme. There is almost no woman in my age who receives her own pension. I'm very thankful for the situation."*

> O.T (72) and her spouse had run a hotel business for approximately 30 years. When they started the business, she was already 40 years old. She was well-off with her own pension and lived in her own single-family home with her eldest daughter's family. *"Immediately after we started, my husband turned our family business into a company. In the post-war industrialization period, without occupational welfare benefits, it was very hard to recruit workers. I also switched my pension plan from the national pension to an occupational one. Also, right after my daughters' graduation from university, we employed them in our hotel business and insured them with occupational welfare schemes. Due to such a wise direction of my husband, his sister, who worked as a kitchen staff in the hotel, also started her own pension plan. For her, it was quite late to start so that she had to contribute retrospectively in order to make up her absent years of the required periods. Now, she lives in a public home for older people with her own pension. Since we employed many other middle-aged to older women, their pension situations were the same as his sister – some had a national pension plan, but started very late; others had never contributed even to the national plan! So, we insured all of them with the occupational plan, and I sorted out any problems with the required contributions. Now, all those women receive their own pension. These women currently in hospital and a nursing*

home are particularly pleased because there are usually no other women who receive pension there. One of them said, 'because I receive a pension, even ¥150,000 [£750] a month, I am not treated badly by the care staff in the nursing home.'"

Women's Changing Views of Welfare

Older Women's Norms and Stigma towards Welfare

In the process of socio-economic change and institutional transition, older women's feelings and attitudes towards state welfare also changed. Perhaps older people in general had never adapted the idea of government as a dominant welfare provider, and thus, the concept of 'the welfare state' had not been firmly established in their minds. Therefore, the dependency of the older women on state welfare had been relatively small, particularly in areas such as personal care, where traditional family norms and values played an important role. Indeed, for this generation, informal exchange of personal care within the family had been common, often predominant, and rather obligatory. The pre-war legal and moral obligations on family support strongly influenced and reinforced the expectations of older people to receive financial and practical support from their adult children.

Due to their normative ideas regarding such family duties, there was a stigma attached to older people claiming or receiving certain types of public welfare, including income maintenance and social services. By stressing family values, the government succeeded in discouraging those people from depending on the state, and kept expenditure on welfare down. In modern society, however, relying exclusively on family support for old age care has become increasingly impractical and problematic. Some younger families appear incapable or unwilling to provide old age care to their parents due to other competing tasks and geographic separation between generations. By the same token, many older people were reluctant to become a burden on their adult children, even though longer life expectancy often requires a greater degree of care and support in old age.

Despite the emerging needs for alternative support, the concept of 'social right' regarding public welfare seemed to be underdeveloped in Japanese society, especially among older people. As a result, older women often placed themselves in an agonizing position: knowing that reliance upon family traditions would not cover their needs adequately, but also facing difficulties adjusting to the changes and in seeking alternative support services. A series of newspaper articles on issues concerning the ageing of society frequently reported the agonies of such older people caught between the assumed social norms and actual practice (*Asahi Shinbun*, 16 to 24 December 1997):

> In the following morning when a community worker visited my bed-ridden mother-in-law, she ordered me in a sharp voice: "Return everything [old-age care related goods such as a bed and a wheelchair] which you borrowed from the welfare office! Stop the public-health nurse's visits as well!" She went on, "that is only for *poor* older people." The community worker's visit seemed to hurt her pride.
>
> When a public health nurse visited an older woman, the nurse was asked to park her car, with 'social welfare office' written on it, far away from the older woman's house. She did not want her to be spotted by the neighbours.
>
> Many families want to bring their older parent home from a nursing home just before he or she dies. To keep up public appearances, they need proof that their parent died at home or at least in hospital, instead of in a nursing home.   (*Asahi Shinbun*, 19 December 1997, p. 29)

Similar views were expressed by the older women in the interviews. Especially for those who could (if pressured) still rely on their adult children for support, receiving certain types of welfare from the state – including care in a nursing home – was seen as shameful or inappropriate practice. For some older people, therefore, it was still the last choice to be cared for by the state, and thus, they pitied others who had no choice but to depend on alternative sources of support besides the family:

> K.H (73) lived with her son and his family in her own single-family home. *"I could never imagine myself moving into a public nursing home. Whenever I have a chance to visit these homes, I always think how pitiful those residents seem."*
>
> N.M (75) divorced her spouse at 57, and moved into a public home for older people when she was 68. She had a married son living in the same city. *"When I broke my hip, I lost income because I couldn't work. Also, I was too young [62] to start collecting basic old age pension. My son offered me the chance to live with his family. But, you know, his*

apartment was too cramped, and I felt uneasy with others. I went to ask the welfare office if I could receive income support. Then, I got to know the staff in the office quite well. A couple of years later, they suggested that I move into a public home for older people. My first reaction was, 'No way! Homes are 'oba-sute-yama' [dumping mountains for older people]³, aren't they. I would never go!' My old image of old folk's homes in pre-war periods was so striking that I broke into tears even thinking about it."

A.A (72) lived in a private purpose-built retirement flat. She purchased a life-estate in the housing development. *"Many people from various backgrounds live in this housing, but mostly, older people from a higher socio-economic background. Surprisingly enough, even former doctors, dentists, and their wives live here. I could not believe it. I used to ask myself why? I still wonder why those people who used to have a respectable career had to move into this housing. You know, even if they let their adult children take over their clinic and house, what's going on [in the family]!? Maybe, they are the people who have modern thinking."*

Responding to the decreasing capacity of conventional family support, the Gold Plan, a new public welfare scheme for older people, was introduced for the development of health and welfare services for older people in 1989. By redefining the family role, the policy emphasis was placed upon care in the community, which brought with it new challenges. Doubts were voiced as to whether sufficient home helps could be found in Japan's labour-short economy; and another was whether older people could adapt to alternative support from outside the family. Culturally, Japanese people tended to have a strong public-private divide over the use of space, as well as degree of physical contact.

Individual houses had been strictly private in Japan, and not usually open to the public, or *tanin*. Thus, unlike some other societies where home visits are more open and casually take place, inviting people into one's own home was not common or well-practiced in Japan. This Japanese characteristic was an obstacle to the fundamental aspect of community care, which was supposed to encourage older people to remain at home and have social services delivered to their home by employed home helps. Also, since Japanese people tended to have little physical/body contact with others in daily life, another obstacle was created. Such attitudes as well as the physical barrier of housing influenced the promotion of the transformation away from conventional family support:

Y.F (74) lived in a rental unit of Silver Housing (public housing for older people provided by the local authority). Her married daughter lived in the same city, and had always provided personal care for her when she needed it. *"Perhaps, because I am still capable of doing most things on my own, I can make this kind of comment. I hate other people such as home helps coming into my house. I don't feel comfortable. I'm very reserved, so I get nervous."*

O.K (77) lived with her son-in-law in their own house. She had provided care to her spouse for six years before he died seven years ago. *"In fact, when my husband became disabled and bed-ridden, the local authority welfare office sent staff every week to bathe him here. At most, four people came! But, in our case, if our young son-in-law could carry him to the bathroom, I could wash him. So, I had enough help at home. Whenever they came, I felt nervous and obliged to serve tea. So, their visits to my house were a burden for me, instead of help."*

K.R (56)[4] had never been married, and lived with her mother and her unmarried younger brother in rental housing. She had been caring for her mother for seven years at home. *"My bed-ridden mother always says that she does not want to die in hospital. Whatever happens, I'm determined to care for her at home. She doesn't like strangers to touch her body. So, I always change her nappies and wipe her bottom each time when she needs it."*

A focus group interview with the middle generation which was conducted as part of the research supported the older women's views and feelings about the issue. Many of these middle-aged women in the interview predicted some difficulties in adjusting to a new physical and social environment to receive care, especially in their old age. For example, moving into different housing would be a major change, and also allowing strangers to come to their house and to provide personal care through physical contact would be another challenge to the social side of their living environments. Due to the cultural orientation (shame-culture) of Japanese people, removing the mental barrier did not seem easy even for younger generations. Indeed, preparing for such a transformation in later life may need more than gradual mental adjustment from earlier periods of conditioning:

"Under such circumstances [if I needed care from strangers], I might have to phone my friend asking, 'A home help is coming tomorrow! Could you please come and clean my house today, before she comes!'"

"Since we can not take our favourite possessions or assets to the next world after death, the most important thing in later life must be good human relationships. Friends and family are important, but these days, we can not rely indefinitely on their support in old age. We certainly need a more established public or private support in a rapidly ageing society."

Transforming Sources and Reliance of Welfare

With more established institutional systems in the 1990s, old age and its related needs and problems seemed no longer to rest merely with the individual or the family. In the research, dependency on state welfare was obvious among older women of a lower socio-economic status. In some cases, family dissolution ruled out the possibility of receiving adequate family support, and thus forced them to seek alternative support. Also, their low income prevented them from purchasing expensive private services. Apart from housing, those people in the state sector were also likely to rely on public welfare more than other groups of older people:

Y.F (72) had been living in a rental unit of Silver Housing (public housing for older people) for 18 months. She had rented an apartment before she moved into the housing. She had one married son. *"Everybody can somehow survive financially these days. Also, [if something beyond your control happens] the state will look after you. That's why it is important for individuals to be as independent as possible. We must do whatever we can do. Otherwise, the state will be bankrupt if everybody depends on it regardless."*

N.M (75) lived in a public home for older people. Her married son and his family lived in the same city. *"I took care of my own parents in the same house until they died. Unlike these days, we were told that we had to look after our parents no matter what burdened us. It was our obligation. When my parents became bed-ridden, there was no established public welfare support or services which we could rely on, either. I had never thought of going to the local authority for help. Our family business as barbers allowed us to survive somehow and look after my parents financially. Well, giving care for older people was still physically hard work, though. Now, I don't want my son to suffer for me, so I'd rather rely on hospital care or public services."*

Some older people had progressive ideas towards alternative and currently available sources of welfare besides family support, and adapted themselves to the evolving welfare systems:

> O.T (72) lived with her eldest daughter's family in her own house. She had cared for her sick spouse on and off for over 30 years by herself. She talked about her sister-in-law's case in relation to improved public welfare services in recent years. *"My sister-in-law is caring for her ageing husband. They do not have children, so do not need to worry about leaving assets to the next generation. Because of their tight cash situation, they decided to sell their own house and moved into public housing. When her husband became disabled, my sister-in-law went to consult with the welfare office and had his needs assessed. Now, he is granted a lifetime use of a bed and a wheelchair from the local authority. My sister-in-law says, 'these days, it's your loss if you don't go to the public welfare office'. He also goes to a day centre to bathe and have a box lunch once a week and pays only ¥500 [£2.50]. During his visit to the centre, my sister-in-law can be freed from her care duty. I didn't know that local authority had become so helpful. It's definitely different from my time."*

> N.H (70) lived with her son's family in their own house. She had looked after her coresident mother-in-law for 14 years until she passed away. She had also looked after her sick spouse for 10 years until he died. Although caring for her mother-in-law was done only by the family members, the situation in her spouse's care was slightly different. *"I currently work as a volunteer in a day centre for older people twice a week. I used to accompany my husband to the centre also twice a week. Most of the time, he was capable of doing things by himself except for a couple of months before he died. But, it was easy for me to take him to the day centre regularly, rather than to care for him exclusively on my own at home. Then, during his visit in the centre, I started helping other clients with eating and bathing. One of the reasons why I started volunteering was that I wanted to repay the debts which my husband owed [by using the services in the centre]. You know, when I looked after my mother-in-law, she didn't go to hospital until the very end; so, we, the family, had to take care of her at home without any outside assistance. If necessary, I would definitely go to a day centre. In this way, it reduces the burden of my coresident family [daughter-in-law]."*

Older people's expectations of receiving care in old age from their adult children are diminishing. Older people began to be aware that relying thoroughly on family support was no longer practical or realistic particularly in the area of personal social care. Instead, the combined sources of welfare, which the public and private services added to the conventional family practice, became a more necessary and preferred form of welfare provision for those women in the research. It was partly due to older people's economic independence with their own income and assets, brought by Japan's post-war economic growth and the development of the social security system. Consequently, such economic independence made it possible for some older people to purchase alternative, higher quality, and more timely services in the private market:

> K.U (71)[5] owned a life-estate in a private purpose-built retirement flat, and had lived there for eight years. She had nephews, but no immediate family members whom she would want to rely on for care. *"If necessary, I would rely on the Gold Plan. A majority of the residents in this private housing have children and a family. But, I think that many of them would prefer to be cared for by the state or the private market, rather than relying on their own family. That's why they are here in this housing. People's attitudes are changing. Since people in this housing development are usually well-off, they would not beg or appeal to their son for help, but be able to live independently by receiving services from this private housing or the state."*

> N.T (74) lived with her eldest son's family in her own house. She socialized mainly with friends of her own age once a week in a 'flower arrangement' class. It was a great pleasure for her to talk with them, or to take a short trip once a month. Among those friends, they talked about many issues affecting an ageing society. *"If I become bed-ridden, I want to be cared for at home, but I don't think that it would be feasible. Even if my daughter-in-law was willing to do so, it would not be possible. So, I would prefer to be hospitalized. Or, if I manage to stay at home, I have to arrange a private home help. I always talk about old age care with my friends, '¥10,000 [£50] for a day – so, we need this much money [gesticulates] to hire a home help for a year.' I expect something from my daughter-in-law, but not everything. It would not be feasible to rely thoroughly on her. Do you think that the number of public home-helpers is enough to meet all our needs? I think that we need more."*

It was not only the limited access and availability of public support, but also the quality of the service provided which was also in question. Unlike a variety of services available in the private market, public support was often likely to be minimal, not 'service'-oriented. Indeed, the universal provision of public welfare for older people had not been the government's aim. Older people in a stronger economic position and people who prefer a higher standard of services were typically expected to purchase welfare services in the private market:

> K.R (56) had been caring for her mother at home. She also received home help services from the local authority. *"As a family carer, I am more willing to care for my mother, and it's easier for me as well. When a home help comes, instead of me relying on home help, I always have to listen to her constant complaints. They complain about their job and colleagues, or their husband's low salary. 'I can't help doing this job because my husband's salary is so low', one says. If they are not really willing to do the job, it's better for them not to come."*

> Both M.H (80) and A.A (72) lived independently in a private purpose-built retirement flat. Some residents in the housing development purchased additional personal services from the private sector. *"Services provided by the local authority are cheap, but your income and needs will be assessed. Usually, someone who lives nearby is sent to help you. If different helpers come each time, it's not good. I don't like it. It's important to have the same person in order to be familiarized with my needs and my flat."* (M.H (80))

> *"But, the private services are too expensive! Somebody told me that ¥10,000,000 [£50,000] will disappear very quickly if you need extensive care services."* (A.A (72))

> *"Cleaning once a week? It's not enough. Some services seem inadequate for me. When my next door neighbour asked about a cleaning service, someone came with a vacuum cleaner in one hand and 'duskin' [a chemical mop] in another, and just vacuumed and wiped at the same time as quickly as she could. I can't stand it if my room is not wiped properly with a wet towel. That's why I've already made arrangement with my [private] home help in case I need more extensive care."* (M.H (80))

In recent years, access to information and the process of applying for available services for older people and the family who care for them had been also significantly improved in many local authorities. For example,

Kitakyushu, where the research was conducted, had set up an 'advisory corner for older people' in each ward office. Through a dedicated help desk, older people can obtain information about any service, and consult with a single member of staff throughout the whole process without being sent around from one help window to another in the ward office. It has reduced the frustration and confusion brought on by heavy-handed bureaucracy, and resulted in a user-friendly environment for older citizens. Public health nurses were appointed to facilitate the consultation process and coordinate between service users and providers. Under this new system, better integration is more likely to be achieved between formerly separated sections of medical, health, housing and welfare to serve older people's needs. In order to provide equal opportunities for people from any social or family background to access the information or available services (and ways of receiving them), public relations will have to play an increasingly important role in the ageing society:

> K.R (56)'s ageing mother had been sick since 1990. Since her mother had a second stroke in 1995, she had been bed-ridden at home. *"The welfare services of the local authority have progressed remarkably since 1990 when my mother first got sick. At that time, on the hospital's advice, I went there to see if they could allocate my mother a special-needs bed. But, they didn't listen to me at all. In 1995, at my second try, their attitude and services were totally different. They were very conscientious, giving me advice and consulting with appropriate people about my situation.... There are still many people who are ignorant about the new public services. I'm trying to spread the information by word of mouth!"*

Concluding Comments

Two broad themes were explored in this chapter. Traditional family support has eroded over recent years, and people have sought alternatives. This shift has not been an easy adjustment for older people who have been brought up with different values and lifestyle expectations. However, the adoption of the view that old age is everybody's concern has highlighted the problems facing older people. In Japan, older people are no longer a minority, or a socially excluded population, but have gained 'silver power'[6]. In the rapidly ageing society, their ever-growing cohorts have become a major influence on the political scene in Japan. Accordingly, the views of older people themselves are becoming more coherent. The issue of an ageing society has been frequently and widely reported on TV programs, newspapers, and other journals in the late 1990s, particularly in the implementation of the Gold Plan. The government's success in raising public awareness may have caused older people to rethink their widely-held perceptions of conventional welfare provision. Consequently, both receiving state support and purchasing private services in the market has become a more acceptable and necessary alternative to traditional family support.

Second, the research revealed significant cases of poverty in old age, particularly among women who lived in state sector housing. Many of these women shared common backgrounds and experiences – often reflecting their marital status, family circumstances, or employment history. A deterioration of the family unit through divorce, separation, or early widowhood often placed those women in a disadvantaged position in the male breadwinner family model of Japan. This was largely related to the post-war employment and welfare systems, which developed on the 'family as a unit' basis. Without a male principal worker in the household, it was difficult for women alone to establish financial stability within the system.

Since the post-war labour market discriminated on the basis of gender, employment opportunities and conditions were also likely to determine women's financial status in old age. The research illustrated how different financial outcomes of women in old age depended on their marital and employment status, One group of women, typically characterized as 'housewives', had not engaged in any paid work, but could be relatively well-off in their own home with their spouse's income and occupational benefits; while another group of women, often single, had worked throughout their adult life, but tended to struggle financially due to a disadvantaged employment status. These contrasts seemed to become more pronounced in their old age. Instead of achieving a more equal society regardless of gender, family background, or employment status, the post-war development of the Japanese welfare state has created inequalities among women according to their marital and employment status.

In the next chapter, further inequalities, such as the wealth gap among families and between genders, are explored through the development of post-war housing policies. In order to highlight the post-war housing supply mechanism, home ownership policies and the unique Japanese practice of company assisted housing programs are analysed. The chapter also examines recent public and private interventions which have emerged in response to new demands in an ageing society, and explores how this policy process has shaped older people's residential choices.

Notes

1   A public non-profit organization supplying subsidized rental units in Japan.
2   Currently junior high school, age between 13 and 15 years.
3   The idea is based on Japanese folklore. Once upon a time, *shogun* established a law whereby older people would be dumped in a mountain when they reached a certain age. The story had a happy ending when *shogun* found out values in older people's knowledge and wisdom.
4   Information obtained through interview with the middle generation. She wanted to speak for her mother.
5   K.U (71) passed away in 21 December 1996, a week after the interview.
6   In Japan, a symbol colour for older people is silver. It is used in many areas such as 'silver seats', priority seats for older people in public transportation. The colour signifies a more positive and respectable image than an otherwise 'drab' gray.

6 Housing and Older People
'Impacts of Housing Policies and Processes'

Introduction

While they are physically, psychologically and socially capable of taking care of themselves, most older people prefer to live and are actually living in houses which are in many ways identical to those of other age groups (Blank, 1988). However, the choice of dwelling for older people may change in response to retirement, widowhood, declining finances and chronic health problems (Golant, 1992). As a person becomes less capable of taking care of herself/himself and starts relying on fixed sources of income such as old age pensions, there are many obstacles and challenges to remaining in the same house and under the same conditions.

Housing fulfils a temporal need for shelter for any age group. Decent and adequate housing is widely recognized as key to sustaining health, dignity and quality of life for all human beings (Hayakawa, 1995; 1997; Hayakawa and Okamoto, 1993; Hoglund, 1985; Pynoos and Liebig, 1995). The critical importance of housing for older people, therefore, originates not only from the idea of a roof over their head, but also from the recognition that housing is closely linked to other physical, mental or social elements. It is essential to have safe, secure, affordable and accessible housing in order to maintain independence. Moreover, older people's housing needs and desires are as diverse as their age, backgrounds, interests, financial status and physical health (Lawton, 1986). Needs change significantly over time as part of the ageing process, and may require constant adjustment rather than a standard fixed solution. Providing older people with various housing options reflecting their changing needs is a critical issue in an ageing society. In view of the rapid demographic changes occurring in Japan and the growing numbers of elderly-only households (apart from traditional extended family living arrangements) in recent years, it is appropriate to examine older people's residential issues in the context of post-war housing policy development.

The Living Situation of Older People: Past and Present

New Trends in Household Structures: Elderly-Only Households

Chapter 2 explained that intergenerational living was a very common occurance in Japan and throughout Asia, and represented the traditional family system. Before the end of the Second World War, almost all older people lived with their children until death, but the ratio has now dropped to approximately 60% in Japan as a whole, and 50% in Kitakyushu where the fieldwork was conducted. In parallel, there has been a remarkable increase in both the number and proportion of elderly-only households in the total households (Table 6.1, Figure 6.1).

According to the *1991 Basic Survey on the Life of People* undertaken by the Ministry of Health and Welfare of Japan, of older people aged 65 years and over: 11.6% lived alone; 27.2% lived as couples; 57.6% lived with child(ren); 3.3% lived with other relatives; and 0.3% lived with non-relatives (the number of older people who were staying in institutional accommodation was excluded) (Ministry of Health and Welfare, 1991). The number of elderly-only households was approximately 800,000 in 1965, which then accounted for only 3.1% of total households. This proportion had increased rapidly to 4,720,000, or 11.6% of total households, by 1991. Both single-elderly and elderly-couple households increased 2.7 times and 3.15 times respectively from 1975. In 2010, approximately one-third of all households will be headed by older people aged 65 and over (Institute of Population Problems, Ministry of Health and Welfare, 1993).

Table 6.1 Number of elderly-only households in Japan (1975-95)

	1975	1980	1985	1990	1995
Households with older people	6,880,921	8,124,354	9,283,983	10,729,464	12,780,231
Elderly-couple households	906,205	1,272,533	1,651,124	2,217,875	3,041,797
Single-elderly households	589,259	881,494	1,180,723	1,623,433	2,202,160

Figure 6.1 Percentage of elderly-only households in Japan (1975-95)

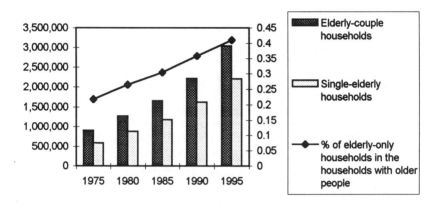

Note: Older people who are living with other older people (relatives or friends) but not as
couples, or who are living in institutional facilities or hospitals are excluded.

Sources: Management and Coordination Agency, Japan. (1985-95), *Kokusei Chousa
[Population Census of Japan]*, Tokyo: Bureau of Statistics; Office of the Prime
Minister, Japan. (1975, 1980), *Kokusei Chousa [Population Census of Japan]*.

Even though the proportion of older people living with their children
increases as they become older and more frail, both the number and
proportion of elderly-only households will continue to increase as society
ages in Japan. These facts underline the growing need to develop suitable
housing options and services which can satisfy the growing number of
elderly-only households.

Home Ownership

Home ownership rates are high in Japan. According to the *1993 Housing
Survey*, 59.8% of Japan's total number of households owned their own
houses (Figure 6.2). This is a relatively high figure when compared with
many other developed societies, aside from England and the US where it was
67.6% and 64.2% in 1991, respectively. These rates, however, are lower in
urban areas. Tokyo, especially, had the lowest at 39.4% in 1993, which was
20% below the national average.

Figure 6.2 Ratio of housing units by tenure in Japan (%) (1963-93)

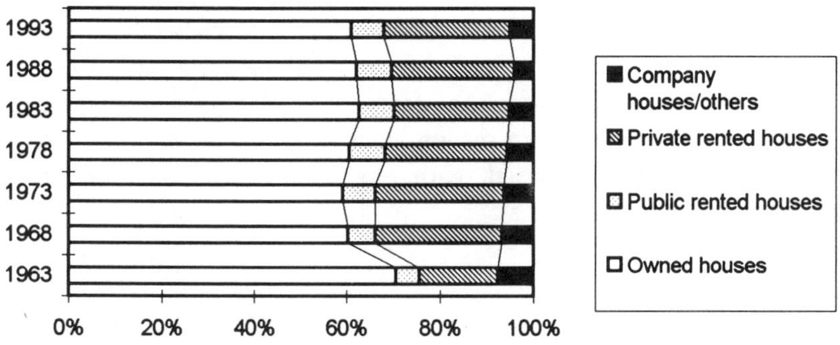

Source: Management and Coordination Agency, Japan. (1963-93), *Juutaku Toukei Chousa [Housing Survey of Japan]*, Tokyo: Bureau of Statistics.

Home ownership rates among households with related members aged 65 years and older are even higher, at 85.7% in 1993; and 84.8% of those lived in single-family homes. In addition, those home ownership rates among older people vary according to their household types. Of extended family households, typically those in which three generations live together, 91.2% owned their own homes, and 90.3% of these lived in single-family homes. Examining which generation actually owns the house serving an extended family is an interesting point. Although many people primarily think of situations where older parents move into their adult children's homes, many of the contemporary arrangements are ones in which the house is owned by the older parents or persons. Due to sky-rocketing land prices and rents, the growth of long distance commuting, and poor living environments in the inner cities, especially in Tokyo, some young couples prefer living in their parents' house rather than struggling to live as a nuclear family (Suzuki, 1989). Suzuki's survey indicated that young couples tended to choose the easiest route to home ownership, often expecting to inherit their parents' house after living intergenerationally. Although older people's home ownership rates are quite high today, especially those of single-family homes, the rates are projected to decrease in the future mainly due to decreased affordability and availability in urban areas.

Among elderly-only households, however, home ownership rates were significantly lower: 83.6% for elderly-couple households and 64.8% for single-elderly households (Management and Coordination Agency, 1993)

(Table 6.2, Figure 6.3). These rates are set to change as the society ages – single-elderly households are more likely to be renters than other households with older family members. The *1993 Housing Survey* also discovered that older home owners were better off, had more floor space, and were more satisfied with their living situations than those in rented accommodation. Even though older renters are insignificant in numbers, they are the ones who are usually poorly housed, with less security, or sometimes require financial or social assistance.

Table 6.2 Number of households with older people by tenure in Japan (1993) (thousand households)

	Owned houses	Public rented houses	Private rented houses	Company houses/ others
Households with older people	10,077	554	1,062	71
Elderly-couple households	2,180	167	245	17
Single-elderly households	1,178	181	448	12

Figure 6.3 Ratio of households with older people by tenure in Japan (1993) (%)

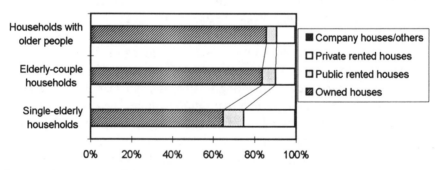

Source: Management and Coordination Agency, Japan. (1993), *Juutaku Toukei Chousa [Housing Survey of Japan]*, Tokyo: Bureau of Statistics.

A Single-Family Home: The Salaried Workers' Dream

The *1993 Housing Survey* showed that single-family homes accounted for 59.2% of all housing in Japan, with the ratio dropping in urban areas. For example, multi-unit structures, such as *manshon* [medium to high-rise condominiums for purchase] and low to medium-rise apartment blocks, accounted for 65% of all housing in Tokyo.

For the older generation, owning a house essentially means owning a single-family home. Over 70% of households with related member(s) aged 65 years and older lived in owner-occupied single-family homes (Management and Coordination Agency, 1990). Aside from those, older people live in other types of housing such as high-rise condominiums, two-storey apartment houses, wooden terraced houses, or a unit in communal housing such as nursing homes. In the inner cities, some older people still live in the older wooden apartments and houses, which were constructed before or immediately after the Second World War, and have not been maintained carefully and need rebuilding (http://www.jinjapan.org/insight/ html/, 1 April 1998). Specially-equipped housing for older people, such as sheltered housing in Britain, is not well developed in Japan. Moreover, the level of access to institutional care (or the amount available) for older people is comparatively low in Japan. Only 2% of older people are institutionalized, compared with other developed countries that range from 4% in Germany to 9% in Sweden (Gibson, 1992).

For post-war generations, *niwa-tsuki ikko-date* [a single-family home with private garden] has been the average salaried worker's dream. A long-distance commute did not stop many workers from purchasing their own home in the suburbs. Seeking a more affordable and spacious house, people move farther and farther away from the inner cities, resulting in uncontrollable urban sprawl. Commuting involves major social costs, especially in the Tokyo region, where commuters usually use trains and must change once or twice (if not more) to get to work. Commuters working in the central section of Tokyo metropolitan area travel an average of 69 minutes to their destinations (Ministry of Transportation, 1990). In extreme cases, some people spend as much as three hours in trains to commute from their single-family home; some commute by a bullet train; and some may occasionally stay in a capsule hotel if they missed the last train home. Even if they are prepared to commute such long distances, purchasing a single-family home in the inner cities has become a distant dream for many people.

Instead, purchasing a unit in a condominium close to a train station has risen in popularity, especially among younger families.

From Quantitative to Qualitative Improvements

Due to war damage, housing shortages were a serious problem in the inner cities immediately after the Second World War. Because the rapid economic growth brought large-scale migration into urban areas, the demand for housing further outpaced the supply. In order to house the growing urban populations, new housing units were built: for example, 257,000 units were constructed in 1955 (http://www.jinjapan.org/insight/html/, 1 October 1997). Since then, the government's focus on supplying large numbers of units has continued. Since 1968, over one million new houses and apartments have been constructed annually under the guidance of the Housing Construction Planning Law. Currently, the number of dwellings exceeds the number of households. In Tokyo, for example, there were 5,300,000 dwellings for only 4,720,000 households in 1993. Thus, the ratio of dwellings to households was 1.1.2 units, and the percentage of vacant dwellings is 9.9% (Management and Coordination Agency, 1993) (Figure 6.4).

Figure 6.4   Number and ratio of dwellings and households in Tokyo (1968-93)   (ten thousands)

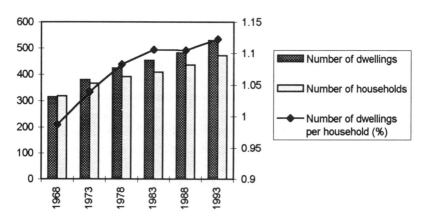

Sources: Management and Coordination Agency, Japan. (1968-93), *Juutaku Toukei Chousa [Housing Survey of Japan]*, Tokyo: Bureau of Statistics.

Although the GNP of Japan is one of the highest of the world, the development of high standard housing and living environment lags behind economic development. Although there is a crude numerical balance between dwellings and households in the inner cities, many houses and apartments are too small, too old, insufficiently equipped, or located in a poor environment (http://www.jinjapan.org/insight/html/, 1 April 1998). Since the late 1960s, therefore, the government's emphasis has shifted from quantitative to qualitative improvements in housing. In terms of housing quality, promoting barrier-free units in housing for older people and people with disabilities has only become an issue in the last decade. Today, many local authorities offer financial assistance to those people for housing adaptation.

In terms of building materials, according to the *1993 Housing Survey*, 34.1% of occupied dwellings in Japan were built of timber, 34% of fireproof timber, and another 31.9% of ferroconcrete or other non-timber materials. There were still surprisingly many out-dated timber dwellings in urban areas. The ratio of new dwellings being built of non-timber materials increased from 37% nationwide in the 1970s to 53% in 1993. The choice of building materials combined with a humid climate can make the life-span of a traditional Japanese-style house very short, compared with that of Western standards. Many dwellings which were built even in the 1960s and 1970s before the current building codes require major renovation (http://www. jinjapan.org/insight/html/, 1 April 1998). Some wooden structures pose threats to the safety of the residents. Safety concerns became even higher after the Great Hanshin Earthquake in January 1995. Older timber houses, in which older people tend to live, are usually beyond their expected life-span.

Due to increased urban land prices and potential rent profits from new buildings as well as for safety reasons, old wooden houses in the market have been targeted for redevelopment into modern multi-unit structures for purchase or rent. The *1988 Housing Survey* showed that about half of the elderly-only households had moved from one rental housing to another rental housing during the previous five years; and the major reason for those moves was eviction or non-renewal of the contract. In many cases, older people cannot afford to move back into new building.

Housing Size

The living space of Japanese dwellings has shrunk since the early 1900s –
the average floor space was 165 square meters, sufficient to accommodate a
large extended family at that time.   Through the process of post-war
reconstruction, smaller houses were built in order to accommodate rapidly
growing nuclear family households, and to supply more houses for the large-
scale urban migration that was occurring as a result of rapid economic
growth.   Only slight improvements have been made since 1979, when a
European Community Commission stated that "Japan was a nation of
workaholics living in what a Western European would only call rabbit
hutches."   The national average floor space per dwelling was 80 square
meters ($254m^2$ for site area) in 1978, which had increased to 92 square
meters ($262m^2$ for site area) by 1993 (Management and Coordination
Agency, 1978; 1993).   In metropolitan areas such as Tokyo, the average fell
to 62 square meters, considerably below the national average.   In order to
further improve the situation, the Construction Ministry has set targets for
housing standards[1] to be met by half of all households by the year 2000,
with tax concessions and low-interest public finance.

   The difference in floor space between owner-occupied housing and
rental housing is significant in Japan: on average, the floor space of owner-
occupied houses is much larger than that of rental housing, company
housing and public housing.   The post-war policies emphasizing home
ownership made possible a remarkable improvement in the size of owner-
occupied houses, which have reached equivalent western standards (Table
6.3).   In contrast, the rental sector has not witnessed such improvements.
The majority remain much smaller (e.g. studio flats, 1DK [one bedroom, a
dining kitchen and a bathroom]) and cater for students or young couples,
compared to the average size in Western societies (Table 6.4).

Table 6.3 International comparison of average floor space (m^2)

	Owner-occupancy	Private rental
Japan (1988)	118.5	40.3
United States (1985)	154.1	112.0
Britain (1986)	81.5	69.7
Germany (1987)	86.3	69.2

Source: Hatta. (1998), *Short-Term Leasehold will Improve Housing Situations in Japan.*

Table 6.4 International comparison of distribution of floor space in private rental housing (%)

	Japan	United States	France	Germany
0-40 m^2	48.4	0.0	0.6	3.1
40-80 m^2	45.6	28.0	47.4	54.9
80-100 m^2	6.0	72.0	52.0	42.0

Source: Hatta. (1998), *Short-Term Leasehold will Improve Housing Situations in Japan.*

Housing Costs

The cost of housing and land in the metropolitan areas is extremely high in Japan compared to other goods and services, and also compared to those in other industrial nations. The value of urban land increased considerably during the high economic growth periods, and particularly during the economic bubble period of the late 1980s.

The post-war housing market is mainly driven by the private sector in Japan. Combined with the low share of state-owned land in urban areas, this tends to push up the price. One of the causes of this recent abnormal rise in land price was the relaxation of land and housing price controls during the Nakasone administration (1982-87), which made the supply of both land and housing dependent on market principles even more than before (Hayakawa and Hirayama, 1991). In 1983, many types of zoning controls were relaxed, and in 1984, the sale of public land began. The land and rent control system was abandoned in 1986, and in 1991 the Housing Rental Law was changed, weakening the rights of tenants. In the 1980s, interest rates were extremely low, so when controls were relaxed, excess capital flowed into land and housing, and those prices rose dramatically (Figure 6.5). In 1989, land prices jumped by 68.6% in Tokyo, and by 46.6% in the three metropolitan areas of Tokyo, Osaka and Nagoya. After the economic bubble burst in the early 1990s, land prices in urban areas have fallen dramatically, and the prolonged recession has kept the market relatively low. Despite the government's recent effort to stimulate the housing market, land prices remain depressed in many regions (http://www.jinjapan.org/insight/html/, 1 October 1997).

Figure 6.5 Average purchase price of housing with land in Japan (1984-95) (ten thousand yen)

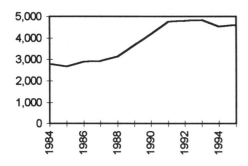

Source: Ministry of Construction, Japan. (1995), *Minkan Juutaku Kensetsu Shikin Jittai Chousa [Survey on the Financial Situation in Private Home Construction]*, Tokyo.

For the average salaried worker in the Tokyo metropolitan area, however, house prices remain far from affordable. In 1988, the average price of a condominium in the Tokyo region was ¥47,500,000 (£237,500); a detached single-family home, nowhere near the luxury detached equivalent in Britain, was ¥50,850,000 (£254,250). These figures equate to 6.9 times and 7.4 times the average annual income, respectively. The national average annual income of those who purchased their houses with land in 1995 was ¥8,764,000 (£43,820) (Ministry of Construction, 1995). In Japan, only 6% to 7% of the total housing is public or co-op housing, while Scandinavian countries such as Sweden have 30% of public housing, the figure rising to 50% if co-ops are included. The post-war policy of owner-occupancy also accelerated the housing price increase and widened the wealth gap between home owners and renters. Achieving restraint and stability in land prices is a top priority for the government (http://www.jinjapan.org/today/html/, 1 April 1998).

The Post-war Housing System: Creating Inequality

Home Ownership

Japan's post-war housing policies have emphasised home ownership. It is based on the idea that housing is the individual's responsibility, a personal problem, and depends mainly on the private market (Hirayama and Hayakawa, 1995). Therefore, the government's direct provision of housing has been minimal. As opposed to the comprehensive housing policies of some European societies, where governments seek to plan and control the total volume of home building (e.g. Germany, Sweden), the Japanese approach is more of supplementary policies (e.g. the US) to provide housing for groups such as low-income earners and older people that could not be served by other sectors (Heidenheimer et al, 1983). It is also related to land policy – Japan's low share of state-owned land in urban areas (approximately 10%) restricts provision of public housing options or proper city planning (Maruo, 1990; 1992).

Only a small amount of public housing for rental (*shiei juutaku*) (4.9% of the total housing supply) has been supplied directly by local authorities with subsidies from the central government, for mainly low-income households. The Japanese Housing and Urban Development Corporation (currently *Juutaku Toshi Seibi Koudan*) was founded in 1955 as a public non-profit organization to supply subsidized rental units (*koudan juutaku*) for urban families. Again, the share of such units in the total housing supply is very small, at 2.1%. Initially, eligibility was limited to family households. Rather than providing housing for life, it served more as a stepping stone to home ownership for younger families. As a consequence, among older renters, 2.2 times as many people live in private rental housing than in public housing.

Government involvement in housing has also focused on the stimulation of housing demand rather than that of housing production (Pynoos and Liebig, 1995). There is no subsidy to both profit and non-profit producers to build good quality rental housing, and there is no housing allowance system except for renters on welfare (e.g. public assistance for living protection). Prospective purchasers are rather subsidized indirectly through a mortgage-guarantee program, low-interest, long-term loans by the Housing Loan Corporation, and tax concessions, usually for owner-occupation. In addition, since the latter half of the 1960s, the housing industry, which has grown through assistance from the government's economic and housing policy, actively began to supply *tateuri juutaku* [built-for-sale housing]. Private financial institutions also began to make housing loans at the same time. Since the late 1970s, the government has continued to promote private home ownership by increasing its financing of the Housing Loan Corporation, as the most cost-effective way to encourage housing investment (Oizumi, 1994). The low commitment by the state to housing provision kept down their expenditure, and resulted in a system of market-driven housing development.   Nevertheless, the housing policy to encourage home ownership faced serious difficulties due to the extraordinary rise of land prices in the bubble economy of the late 1980s (Oizumi, 1994).

Home ownership has brought many additional advantages. First, it played an important role in improving the housing conditions during the process of post-war housing reconstruction in Japan (Hirayama and Hayakawa, 1995). Especially in tight rental housing markets with relatively poor housing stock in urban areas, for renting families to be able to improve their housing conditions, home ownership remains the best option. Second, home ownership provides security and stability which are often lacking in Japanese rental markets. Owning one's own home or condominium reduces the fear or threat of being evicted and provides greater stability in later life. Third, home ownership may grant continuity (tradition and wealth accumulation) to the family. It fulfills the traditional Japanese practice of passing on a house and land as accumulated family wealth in the form of dwellings to the next generation. It also provides a greater opportunity to form an extended family household than rental housing. Owned houses are usually larger and can accommodate an extended family, and it is a cost-effective option for both parties. Also, home ownership offers a coresident younger couple the likelihood of inheriting the house after living intergenerationally. Finally, home ownership has cultural dimensions such as social status (Dupuis and Thorns, 1996). A Japanese saying, '*ie wo motte ichinin-mae*', indicates that home ownership gives younger people, usually the male head of the household, social recognition and 'approval' as a full adult.

On the other hand, in Japan, as many other industrial societies, the post-war development of home ownership can be seen as processes of social restratification (Forrest and Murie, 1995). It certainly played a role in creating inequality and a wealth gap among families, and between home owners and non-owners. Since home ownership has a strong tendency and characteristics for asset formation in Japan, family wealth is often accumulated by inheriting housing and land (Hirayama and Hayakawa, 1995). While home-owning families can further increase their assets over generations, the chances of low-income renters becoming home owners are slim. This also places them in a disadvantaged position for creating family assets. The wealth gap between home owners and renters is therefore likely to widen over time.

According to the *1989 Basic Survey on the Life of People*, the economic situation of older people was relatively good. The discrepancy between high-income persons and low-income persons was, however, greater among older people than the national average – while there was a small number of very wealthy older people, there was a large group of low-income older people (Maeda, 1993). Their income reflects their status as home owner. Those low-income people are, therefore, likely to be renters. Since the emphasis on home ownership has kept the rental sector very small (see Table 6.2), the policies have constrained the residential choices of low-income renters.

It is said that "tenants have very strong rights in Japan – under the Civil codes, tenants have vested rights and cannot be forced out without good cause (e.g. an owner moving back to live in the house); and since rent increases have to be mutually acceptable, rental payments by long-situated tenants are low" (Patrick and Rohlen, 1987). In reality, however, for renters, especially older renters on a fixed pension, the threat of rent increases is a constant worry. Since older people tend to occupy older accommodation which is likely to be replaced with modern buildings, eviction may be another serious threat. According to the *Housing Survey* between 1979 and 1983, the percentage of elderly-headed households who gave eviction as the reason for having to move was 24%, compared to a 9.5% national average in Japan. Surprisingly, forced eviction can happen in public housing, when low-income renters fail to pay their rents due to changing circumstances such as unemployment, reduced income by retirement, or rent increases. In 1996, over 4,000 lawsuits were brought against those renters in public housing who had failed to pay rent over a three-month period – in 1,325 cases, tenants were forced out, and the numbers continue to increase (Hayakawa, 1997). There were even some tragic cases where the threat of eviction (or the desperation felt by losing accommodation) drove older tenants to commit suicide the day before their legal occupancy ended (*Asahi Shinbun*, 3 July 1992). Additionally, older people, especially lone renters, are often discriminated against as a potential problem (e.g. starting fire, death) by property owners and estate agencies (Hayakawa, 1979; 1993). Indeed, tight rental stocks, frequent rent increases, and discrimination against older renters by property owners make remaining in the same house or moving within the rental sector for older tenants very difficult and problematic.

Despite the harsh rental regimes facing older people, recent political debates are moving towards deregulating the current Leasehold Act by increasing the rights of property owners. The expression, 'short-term leasehold' has been proposed to give property owners the right to refuse an extension of a contract (usually after two years) without any reason. The proposed legal change is supported by some economists and developers. It is believed that such deregulation will encourage an expansion of rental stocks (especially larger-size housing),[2] decrease rents, and ease the existing burden on property owners who make up the short fall of public sector housing (Abe et al, 1997; Hatta, 1998). It may also stimulate the economy through urban redevelopment. The social needs and protection of renters are, however, largely excluded from these arguments. Stability in the rental sector is likely to be reduced, which may make it more difficult for those renting with a family to plan their future or establish a life in a community (Harada, 1998; Hayakawa, 1997). Without further public assistance (e.g. rent subsidies, public housing provision), the cost of any transfer will likely fall on the low-income renters themselves.

Occupational Welfare: Company Housing

In Japan, company housing as a part of occupational welfare also had a unique role in the development of the post-war housing system. During the periods of economic growth, some companies constructed housing such as apartment blocks and dormitories to accommodate their employees, with highly subsidized rents. Others leased accommodation from either the private sector or from relocated employees for the same purpose. The average level of the rents for company housing was about one-third of the rate for public housing, and one-tenth of the private renting in 1982 (Fujita, 1984). Of the conventional components of occupational welfare, housing assistance has been, in terms of cost, by far the most important voluntary service provided by companies. The scale of the assistance varied depending upon the size of the companies: the largest accounting for up to half of the total occupational welfare expenditures for the largest firms, but considerably less for the smaller firms (the average was 40%) in the 1980s (Nihon Chingin Kenkyu Centre, 1985). This enterprise initiative was a reflection of the need for greater geographical flexibility in workers' mobility and relocation during the periods of high economic growth. On the other hand, it had the effect and the purpose of tying workers to the company during those periods (Kamata, 1984). It was additionally a reflection of the high cost and shortage of housing in many industrial areas. Securing affordable housing through their companies gave a great incentive to workers to stay in a particular company. Indeed, company housing filled the gap between public and private housing provision, and created its own role and position within the post-war Japanese housing system.

Company housing had been used for many workers as a bridge to home ownership. One of the advantages of living in company housing was to enable sufficient money to be saved to achieve home ownership. Many people in the generation who had regular full-time employment in larger companies made a relatively smooth entry to home ownership. In the early periods of economic growth, workers often used their lump sum retirement allowance to purchase a home. Over the last couple of decades, however, sufficient capital was able to be raised from the company with the assistance of the private sector finance for purchasing a house while they were still employed (ILO, 1982). For example, in the case of Hitachi, 38% of households headed by a male worker were living in company housing in 1967. A decade later this figure had fallen to 27% while the rate of private home ownership had risen from 44% to 62% in the same group (ILO, 1982). Nowadays, most young recruits in Hitachi can still expect dormitory accommodation, and some married couples live in some form of company housing. However, not all employees wish to live in company housing, and resources have gradually shifted into assisting employees to purchase their own housing, mainly via home loans or subsidized interest payments (Hall, 1988). Promoting home ownership through company saving schemes geared to home purchase and low-interest loans also benefits companies themselves by raising funds through employees' savings (Ohmoto, 1996).

Like other welfare benefits, the distribution of company housing was not a universal benefit for workers (see Chapter 4). Company housing benefited those in the more privileged sectors of the workforce and in the major firms (Gould, 1993). Considering that only 23.3% of employees were engaged by private firms with over 100 employees, 19.9% by firms of between 30 and 99 employees and the remaining 56.8% engaged in small firms with under 30 employees in 1987 (Office of the Prime Minister, 1987), it is evident that the privileged were a small group of workers. Moreover, access for single-female and female-headed households to occupational welfare including housing assistance was, again, much less equal than for male-headed households. This often resulted in excluding those households from home ownership, and thus wealth accumulation in the form of dwellings in later life. As a result, being *female*, *single*, and *old* can be a triple-setback to obtaining decent housing.

New Policy Initiatives: Filling a Gap?

Japan did not have particular housing policies for older people at the beginning of the post-war period, thus general housing policies were used to cover the housing needs of the older population. Gradually, newer and greater demands for both services and housing for older people began to be recognized by policy makers and interest groups as a result of the rapidly ageing society. This section examines three particular issues: firstly, what are the important criteria which affect older people's choice of residence?; secondly, how much are their needs and desires met through new public and private initiatives?; and thirdly, who are the people still badly served by current housing supply?

Promoting Staying-Put Schemes

To a certain extent, the expansion of elderly-only households and the decreasing rates of coresidency reflect older people's growing preference for independent living. Some people choose to grow older in their own community since they place great value on being in a familiar neighbour-hood. Many prefer to remain in the same house even if the accommodation lacks basic comforts and conveniences. The decision to remain in a familiar neighbourhood may also reflect the desire to continue (or to maintain) existing relationships and social networks with relatives and friends. In addition, a 'natural' helping network between neighbours tends to develop quickly in existing communities (Rice and Bain, 1986). Moving to unfamiliar neighbourhoods in old age can cause serious mental distress, as well as affecting and speeding up physical deterioration (Hayakawa, 1993; Ito et al, 1994). Integration with the community tends to promote healthier, more normal lives for older people, and gives them a feeling of satisfaction and meaning to life. In many cases, however, physical and financial limitations mount as age increases, making it difficult for older people to remain in the place in which they currently reside.

Due to the traditional heavy reliance on family resources, community care services and facilities to promote older people's independent living have been consistently underdeveloped in Japan. It was not until the late 1980s when a national guideline was finally set up to respond to the emerging needs of an ageing society, in which nearly one in four Japanese would be 65 or over by the 2020s. In December 1989, the Japanese government, under the agreement of three ministries (Ministry of Health and

Welfare, Ministry of Finance, and Ministry of Home Affairs), promulgated the Gold Plan:

> ... [it emphasized the] need to create a longevity-welfare society of bright vitality in which citizens can be assured of living out a healthy and meaningful life. Therefore, based on the goals of introducing the consumption tax, we will move forward in building up provision of public services in the area of health and welfare for older people.
>
> (Ministry of Health and Welfare, 1990: pp 52, 210-211)

A total expenditure of over 6 trillion yen (about 30 billion pounds) was planned for the following 10 years. All municipalities and prefectures in Japan were also obliged to comply with 10-year long-term plans for the health service and welfare of older people. The main thrust of the Gold Plan was a 'staying-put approach', to improving services and facilities for older people to remain at home, through strengthening services such as home help, increasing the provision of day care centres, and short-stay facilities, rather than costly institutional development. According to this plan, before the year 2000, the number of home helps was to be increased from 31,405 (1989 figures) to 100,000; the number of day care centres for older people from 1,080 to 10,000; and the number of skilled nursing homes from 182,019 beds to 240,000 beds. Under the plan, the quality of life of frail older people and the families who care for them would be significantly improved from its present level. A common criticism of the plan was, however, that the target numbers were still too small, noting, for example, that the level of services planned for the year 2000 would still be lower than the current level of such services in many Western European countries (i.e. only about one-fifth the number of home helps in Denmark) (Ogawa and Retherford, 1997). Also, total spending on all these community-based services was only about a quarter of the long-term hospitalization costs of bedridden older people (*Asahi Shinbun*, 30 December 1989). In December 1994, the Gold Plan was amended to a higher level, called the New Gold Plan, with more realistic and feasible target numbers.

Local authorities have also been taking initiatives to promote older people's independent living. For example, Edogawa-ward, Tokyo, has established a model scheme of housing adaptation programs which provides unlimited subsidies to any household with older family member(s) without eligibility restrictions; and Kitakyushu started operating 24-hour home help services in the early 1990s. Such staying-put schemes are widely practised in Scandinavian countries, where after several years of study and debate, authorities decided to stop building more nursing homes and instead, to rely on a variety of residential housing types with services to meet older people's needs (Pynoos and Liebig, 1995). The strengths of the approach are to offer older people residential choices by separating housing assistance and services rather than packaging them together, and to enhance the possibility of remaining in the same housing. If, however, their accommodation is lacking stability, accessibility, affordability, or supportive features such as barrier-free designs, this strategy to deliver social services to their own home will not be feasible or effective.

Promoting Intergenerational Living

It has been argued that the steady decline of extended family living over the past decade of rapid economic growth is a temporary one or a mere postponement of coresidency (Hashimoto, 1992; 1993) – commonly, the new nuclear family plans for their older parents to move into their household at a later stage in the life cycle (e.g. at retirement, widowhood, illness). Since community-based care systems as the alternative means to family support for older people are still inadequate, this trend of an emerging extended family in later life may continue. On the other hand, starting coresidency with a change of life cycle in later life is relatively difficult since both generations and households have already established lifestyles and social circles (Hayakawa, 1993; 1995). Therefore, increasing numbers of older people are also reluctant to coreside with their adult children even after a change of personal circumstances. Whether the trend is temporary or a substantive change, recent public and private interventions are encouraging such traditional family living arrangements, perhaps with the intention of shifting some responsibilities back to the family.

Extended family living is still the dominant form of provision for older people, and the government views Japan's pattern of living arrangements as a unique asset (Ogawa and Retherford, 1997). Coresidency certainly provides a perfect venue for informal care provision among family members. Since the 1980s, both the Ministry of Construction and the Ministry of Health and Welfare have begun to focus on housing policies directed at extended family living, which is designed to preserve the traditional system of family support (Campbell, 1992). In support of the Construction Ministry's effort, a new type of housing for five-person three-generation family called a 4LLDK (4 bedrooms, 2 living rooms, a dining-kitchen and a bathroom) was introduced into public housing. The number of such units is, however, still very limited. In addition, the Housing Loan Association has introduced the 'two-generation housing loan', a loan inheritance system over generations. Under this system, two generations can obtain a longer repayment period to purchase a house which serves extended family living. Private loan organizations also follow suit, using this system to expand the scope of housing loans. Furthermore, older parents as well as younger persons, who coreside with older parents or relatives, have their taxable income reduced. Again, these new initiatives strongly favour home-owning families with various types of financial assistance.

The private sector is also promoting a new type of extended family living. This new product of the Japanese housing industry called *ni-setai juutaku* [two-household housing] is detached housing, planned on the presumption that older parents coreside with their adult children. One of the major reasons for decreasing rates of coresidency has been the drawback of such living arrangements. The close physical proximity of different generations (especially, older mother and her daughter-in-law), each with their own needs, desires, lifestyles and preferences, often led to conflict within the extended family. This problem has been reduced with the new design allowing for the creation of two separate households, with separate amenities and facilities, all under one roof. However, *ni-setai juutaku* is not the same as semi-detached housing in the West – there is still some consideration and desire for human interaction within the house, and they usually have connecting doorways or interphones joining the two different living spaces. Nowadays, almost all of the major private homebuilding companies have such schemes. Sales have increased rapidly in recent years, often with the rebuilding of existing houses owned by older parents. For example, the proportion of two-household housing to single-family homes supplied in 1991 was estimated at over 40% for the whole of Japan and about 50% for Tokyo (*Asahi Shinbun*, 23 January 1992). For many young couples, it has become an unrealistic dream to purchase a single-family home in metropolitan areas such as Tokyo. Therefore, the cooperation of two generations to combine family household income is viewed as a practical way to achieve the goal of home ownership.

Promoting these traditional arrangements by utilizing family resources for care-giving seems in many ways a cost-effective option for the government to minimize the funding of older people in a rapidly ageing society. The state's direct provision of housing can be kept to a minimum. However, fundamental socio-economic changes, as well as changes in values, are eroding the capacity, ability and willingness of the Japanese family to provide care for older parents (Ogawa and Retherford, 1997). It is uncertain whether these initiatives will be able to slow down the rapid increase of elderly-only households. In traditional families, where daughters-in-law in particular look after older parents(-in-law), many may find it difficult to survive. As more women join the labour market for paid work, the geographical distance between generations created by high educational and occupational mobility increases and the trend towards family nuclearization continues. Also, older people's growing preference to maintain freedom and independence is another significant factor. For example, the survey conducted in Kitakyushu in 1992 on housing supply for older people indicated that for the city's older population, coresiding with their adult children or moving into institutions are no longer the top choice (City of Kitakyushu, 1992). On the other hand, older people's growing worries concerning health and living conditions are inevitable in the process of ageing. The results indicated another shortcoming of the policies. The proposed supply of supportive or intermediate housing options (between full independence and institutions) still seems insufficient to meet the needs of low to middle-income older people who are semi-independent.

Expanding Housing Options for Older People

In response to new and growing demands for independent living by older people, there have been both publicly-funded and privately-sponsored 'supportive housing'[3] projects operating in Japan since the late 1970s. Linking housing with social services has finally become an issue in Japanese housing policy and practice for older people. This type of housing is a practical solution when independent living, or living with either a family or an extended family with different age groups, is undesirable or impossible for physical, emotional, or financial reasons. European examples also suggest innovative directions for the improvement and selective implementation of supportive living arrangements as an important response to semi-independent older people who must move from their own homes, but who do not require institutionalization (Chellis et al, 1982).

Consequently, coordination of two ministries (Ministry of Construction and Ministry of Health and Welfare), or two equivalent departments in local authorities, has become necessary to make more efficient use of resources, to articulate older people's needs for living, and to avoid a duplication of programs. In 1985, the Construction Ministry with the Ministry of Home Affairs also moved in a more innovative direction to develop regional plans for housing, centering on public housing projects with social services, recreational, and even health care facilities attached. In addition, since the late 1980s, local authorities have started developing supportive housing for low-income to middle-income older renters reflecting national guidelines. Their initiatives were met through the provision of 'Silver Housing', which was marketed as public housing for rent to provide physically independent older people with barrier-free housing design and care services (e.g. a life-support advisor). The housing is also coordinated with a day care centre; and the funding of a 'Care House', a type of housing project which evolved from one type of nursing home and came to more closely resemble ordinary housing with social assistant systems. Although 19 'Silver Housing' projects had been approved in various local authorities by 1989 and numbers are predicted to increase, this costly project to serve a smaller group of older people seems to have lower priority within the limited resources of many local authorities.

The housing industry in Japan has also been active in providing multi-unit purpose-built housing for older people to purchase since the late 1970s. These private housing complexes are gradually increasing in number and quality, and are likely to offer a wide range of independent services for older residents such as a dining room for group meals in addition to individual kitchenettes; an emergency alarm system; 24-hour front service; communal facilities such as lounges and activity areas; and organized social activities. Usually, no in-site skilled nursing or medical care is offered. There were approximately 178 such facilities throughout Japan in 1992 (Ministry of Health and Welfare, 1992b). However, these projects currently serve only affluent older people, since they usually require an initial large lump sum to purchase the 'life-estate'[4], and a monthly fee for management and operation. These projects are currently relatively large in scale since services for older people such as meal provision and human assistance could only be provided effectively and efficiently when there was a centralized and concentrated population (Ito and Sonoda, 1994). However, since those projects have not yet proved to be economically viable for both parties, there are difficulties in filling up the spaces (for example, the current vacancy rates for two projects in Kitakyushu are as high as 20% to 30%) (City of Kitakyushu, 1992).

In addition, during the late 1980s, before the Japanese economic 'bubble' burst, the Ministry of Health and Welfare initiated the 'Well Ageing Community (WAC) project', which was supposed to fill the gap of costly housing developments, with public and private partnerships. These projects also faced severe financial constraints after the economic bubble burst in the early 1990s:

> ... Ten out of thirteen local authorities, whose plans had already received approval for the national government's funding, announced the cancellation or postponement of the projects. The main reason for revising the plans is that they estimate the projects, especially congregate housing projects which require huge amounts of strata fees, would be very unlikely to attract enough older clients to make the projects economically feasible.   (*Asahi Shinbun*, 28 July 1994, p. 1)

Alternative housing to reflect the diverse needs, preferences, and financial backgrounds of older people beside traditional extended family living is still underdeveloped in the Japanese housing system. Both new provision of such housing and the adaptation of existing dwellings to suit older people's housing needs are required to be cost-effective options.

In order to utilize the existing resources to accommodate those elderly-only households, one long-term goal of the Construction Ministry was to allow single-person households into public rental housing provided by the Housing and Urban Development Corporation. The policy was initially introduced in 1979. Compared with contemporary standards, these rental units of public housing, built in the first two decades of the post-war period, are of remarkably low-quality. Some 30,000 such units were hard to let in the late 1980s because of their poor facilities, poor state of repair, and extremely small unit size (many units are 2DK [2 bedrooms, a dining-kitchen and a bathroom]; and some even 2K [2 rooms, a kitchen and a bathroom]). As Japanese society became more affluent and younger families demanded more living space, the attraction of this housing became its subsidized (and low increases in) rent and relatively secure tenure for single-elderly and elderly-couple households. Nowadays, due to relaxed regulation and because these units are too small, too old, and insufficiently equipped, many of those projects are gradually becoming 'housing for older people' (*Asahi Shinbun*, 9 April 1997). It is not surprising to find low-income older renters occupying these subsidized rental units often in a very poor state of repair.

Preventing Social Institutionalization

Until the 1980s, apart from extended family living, institutional living such as nursing homes was the only option available for older people who needed physical or financial assistance, but could not or did not want to rely on their family or friends. Historically, this dates back to the *Meiji* period when the first homes for older people, *yourouin*, were established by private charity workers to provide relief facilities. Public responsibility did not emerge until 1932 when the Poor Relief Law was enacted to provide legal support for those homes. Since then, there have been many legal amendments made to improve the welfare of older people. However, due to these historical ties, financial difficulties are still considered a necessary pre-condition for eligibility to such contemporary nursing homes (Okamoto, 1996). Despite the limited privacy in many nursing homes where a shared room with two to six people is still common, moving into such homes is not an easy option for many older people since demand exceeds supply and because eligibility restrictions are strongly enforced.

In addition, not only were the quality and quantity of such institutions insufficient, but they also tended to be built in undesirable locations, thus segregating older people from the rest of society and severing their social contacts. In the process of ageing, declining health, retirement, loss of a spouse or significant friends, fear of crime, and displacement due to rental eviction can result in growing isolation and loneliness for many older people. Without adequate support services in the community, these factors may contribute to individuals becoming more physically, socially and financially vulnerable than is warranted (Granger and Kaye, 1991), often resulting in premature and unnecessary institutionalization.

Social hospitalization, where older people stay in hospitals for lengthy periods without critical medical conditions, is a unique phenomenon found among Japanese older people, the downside of underdeveloped community care and inadequate housing provision (Kose, 1990). The average length of stay in hospitals and other inpatient institutions is appreciably longer in Japan than in other industrial societies. It was 45 days for Japan in 1990, compared with only 10 days for the US in 1983, 13 days for France in 1987, and 20 days for Sweden in 1987 (Health and Welfare Statistics Association, 1994; OECD, 1990). Length of hospitalization among older people is even longer than these average figures – 79 days in 1990 for people aged 65 years and older. One reason why older people in Japan tend to have such lengthy stays in hospital is the structure of copayments under the social security system (medical plan).

In the late 1990s, copayments for intermediate care nursing homes were ¥60,000 (£300) per month, compared with ¥39,000 (£195) for hospitals, despite the fact that the costs to the government were much higher for hospitals (Ministry of Health and Welfare, 1995). Also, hospital beds are more readily available than nursing home beds. Raising copayments for hospital care appears to offer considerable potential for reining in hospital costs as the availability of intermediate care nursing facilities increases. Expanding the number of intermediate nursing homes, which are intended to serve as way-stations between hospital and home, would be one solution in order to reduce pressure on hospitals, which currently provide considerable long-term care for older people at a high cost to the government. More fundamental improvements in living environments (e.g. housing adaptation) are also needed to prevent such unnecessary hospitalization since it is not only associated with medical reasons, but also many cases can be attributed to social reasons such as fragmented family relations, financial problems, or inadequate housing. Current social pressure to expect unconditional family support for older parents tends to create tension between generations. Older people's reluctance to leave hospitals is strongly associated with the family function and their residential situation when adult children are physically, financially or emotionally incapable or unwilling to support their older parents.

Concluding Comments

The rapidly ageing society has created greater demand for new types of housing and services for older people in Japan. Particular importance should be placed on bridging the gap between the wishes of older people to live as independently as possible for as long as possible, and their increasing worries over declining health and financial conditions. Promoting traditional coresidency through new housing designs and financial arrangements is one response. Expanding the housing options open to older people with both public and private initiatives is another. Despite the great demand, intermediate housing for older people (between traditional coresidency with adult children and institutions) is, however, still in short supply in Japan. Yet, current government policies for housing for older people are moving directly towards improving the staying-put (community care) schemes, in line with international trends. Due to the underdeveloped nature of Japan's social services and its shortage of appropriate housing stock, it is unlikely that the country will be able to keep pace with the solutions and systems adapted by other industrial societies, particularly considering Japan's rapidly increasing older population.

Not every older person currently resides in their ideal housing. Due to the post-war policy emphasis on home ownership, housing conditions and choices are much worse for renters than home owners. Since accumulation of family wealth is often made through home ownership, wealth gaps between owners and non-owners are likely to be widened. As a result, low-income older people are likely to be renters. In addition, whether home owners or renters, moving into more suitable housing in old age poses great difficulty due to limited public provision, costly alternatives in the market, and property owners' discrimination against older renters. Moreover, single females or female-headed households cannot have access to quality housing as equally or as easily as male-headed households. Indeed, being female, single and old, as well as a renter, represents probably the worst combination of factors.

Such housing choices and constraints for older people were further examined in the fieldwork. The women expressed their individual views and values, often stressing the importance of owning a house. The process of home ownership for women is also analysed in the next chapter, contrasting the situations of non-home owners. Following the transformation of family traditions examined in Chapter 3, the next chapter further investigates the factors which have influenced and even constrained their residential choices.

Notes

1   In the case of an urban apartment for a four-person household, the target is a total area of 91 square meters with three bedrooms, a living room, a bathroom and a dining-kitchen area.

2   Under the current Act, it is assumed that many property owners are reluctant to lease their house because of the risk and uncertainly of tenants' 'squattering' their house forever.

3   Supportive housing for older people is defined as types of housing planned and designed to meet the special needs of older people through design and service provision. It assists them in maintaining a (semi-)independent lifestyle and prevents unnecessary institutionalization as they grow older. It often offers communal meals, and a warden.

4   Life-estate is the right to occupy a property for the period of one's natural life. Thereafter, it would revert to the project owner.

7 Women and Housing Choices

Introduction

The older women who were interviewed for the fieldwork either coresided with their adult children or lived alone. These single-elderly households were further divided into two categories – women who lived independently with their own finance in the market sector housing; and women who lived on state benefits including residency in a public home or a Silver Housing project. Focusing on these three housing (welfare) sectors served the purpose of differentiating the relevance of factors such as their socio-economic status, housing tenure and type and degree of family support and relations (both with their spouse and with their adult children). Almost all of the informants in the family sector lived in an owner-occupied single-family home, either owned by themselves or their adult children (sometimes after a transfer of the ownership). Most of the informants in the market sector were also chosen from home owners for the purpose of drawing a clear distinction from low-income renters in the state sector. This was designed to aid analysis of the issues which were raised in the previous chapter and to enable comparisons of the older residents across the three sectors.

Importance of Home Ownership

Given the national government's emphasis on home ownership, what did owning a house mean to these older individuals? In the research, the women's beliefs and attitudes towards home ownership were not only the result of such government control, but also strongly linked to their traditional orientation and cultural identity. This first section, therefore, looks at the women's views on home ownership – the reasons why it was considered to be a necessity or common practice. Using the older women's words, this section also illustrates the problems associated with traditional aspects of home ownership.

Security of Tenure

Security of tenure was highly valued in home ownership as a critical element of housing as shelter. The importance of this element is universal for any age group:

> N.T (74) and her spouse had always owned their own house. At the time of the interview, she lived with her eldest son's family in her own single-family home. *"Rental housing is a nuisance in that you have to pay rent every month, and rely on someone else's decision.... In our generation, we used to say that we wouldn't give our daughters away to anyone without his own house. If she married to the family who owned a house, she as the younger generation would get [inherit] the house later on. If you thought about your children's security, you had to make sure of that."*

As a result of post-war housing policies, including the re-evaluation of urban land, the growth of the rental sector has been kept minimal. For post-war generations, therefore, home ownership has served as an essential and almost single pathway to secure decent housing. The research found that especially for older women with fixed income such as pensions, secure tenure provided stability for their residential living in old age. It further protected them from external threats and uncertainties such as rent increases and eviction faced in the rental sector:

> K.U (71) moved into a private purpose-built retirement flat in the late 1980s. She purchased the life-estate of the housing so that she was able to remain in the housing for the rest of her life. *"I was living in Tokyo right after the War. In Tokyo at that time, it was common to live in rental housing. In contrast to the housing situation now, even among single-family homes, there were many rental housing units available. But, the situation has changed over time – I had been very much aware what my own housing situation was going to be like in the future [in her old age]. So, in order to secure my residential living, I started looking for an appropriate private housing for older people for purchase in my 50s when such developments were first introduced in the market."*

From a Japanese perspective, important elements of residential stability included obtaining a so-called 'home for life' or 'family residence' in which the family was committed to remain in the same owner-occupied housing for life. Thereafter, it would frequently pass on to the younger generation. This situation differs from societies such as Britain where people moved within the owner-occupied sector more frequently and flexibly:

> O.T (71) and her spouse had moved four times before they decided to have their own house built. *"Since we were fed up with moving from one rental house to another, I felt that it was time to settle down in one place. We also knew that my husband would not have any more 'tenkin' [a transfer by a firm]. That's why we decided to have our own house built. Once we owned a house, we were not supposed to move again."*

Family Continuity

Home ownership had a major role in accumulating family wealth over generations, which symbolized family continuity in Japan. Even for an average Japanese family, it served as a crucial means to maintain family tradition and continuity with accumulated wealth in the form of dwellings obtained through inheritance. Compared to those traditional families with normative ideas and practices, therefore, people without their own (or adopted) children tended not to have such a strong incentive to obtain or maintain their family residence:

> S.Y (74) was only 20 years old, when she divorced her spouse six months after her marriage. Although she had once owned her own house, she handed it to her coresident sister's family and moved out to live in rental housing on her own. She had no children from her marriage. At the time of interview, she lived in rental housing provided by the Housing Corporation. *"I no longer have an attachment to the idea of owning my own house. The life ahead of me is very short, so there's no point in owning a house from now. There is really no point because I don't even have a successor [adult children who inherit a house], either."*

Sometimes, home owners had less flexibility when moving in response to changing needs than those renters. Since inheriting ownership of a family residence also included geographical continuity in the sense that the successive younger generations were expected to remain in the same location (property), selling a home sometimes meant breaking family continuity. In modern society which involves high occupational-related mobility, however, keeping such a tradition has often proved impractical or problematic. Because of the tradition, some older women were tied to their own home even after the housing became inadequate for them to live in. Also, adult children, who lived away from their older parents or had already owned their own house in a different location, were sometimes placed in an agonizing position, whether they should have sold the inherited family tradition:

> M.S (82) had been a renter throughout her marriage. *"If you owned a house, you were tied to it. The house would get too big to manage for an old couple, but you couldn't easily trade down or sell it to move into an adult child's house because you owned 'the' house. I've heard of many cases where adult children didn't let their parents sell it. Being a renter, I was able to move into my son's house very smoothly."*

> One year after her spouse's death, M.H (80) moved a long distance (from Kyoto to Kitakyushu) to live in a private purpose-built retirement flat, located close to her son's family. Even though she had no intention of moving back to her house in Kyoto anymore, she had not sold the house yet. *"It's no use owning a house somewhere you can not live. Since all my husband's siblings live around the house, I couldn't dare sell it. If I sold it, what do you think they would say. I'm sure that they would say, 'when her husband died, she even sold the house!' I can't face their criticism. It's so unreasonable since his grave is here, though...."*

> K.T (80) thought that home ownership combined with family tradition caused only a problem these days. *"My distant relative died recently at the age of 86 after having lived in her own single-family home independently for years. All her children were at some point transferred by their company to far-away cities and eventually bought a house there. Today is nothing like the past time when the eldest son used to take over 'Ie' and reside in their family residence. Children leave their old parents and buy a house wherever they go. Look, there are lots of houses around here left empty after older occupants died. Their children seem not to know what to do with them."*

Intergenerational Living

Home ownership also had positive impacts on maintaining traditional living arrangements. Rental housing was usually smaller in size and lower in quality (see Chapter 6), and owner-occupied housing was more likely to provide a venue to promote traditional intergenerational living arrangements. Thus, it helped to retain family continuity. In addition, coresidency in an owned home often made generational transfer of family assets easier:

> O.K (77) lived in an owner-occupied single-family home with her son-in-law. *"Right after the War, our first company housing was a wooden terraced housing. We had two tiny rooms and a little kitchenette. It was enough for the three of us [parents and a small child] at that time, though. Then, I started moving around with my husband who worked in various construction sites. When my only daughter had a baby, I really started missing them, and longing for a 'stable home'. I'd been living in rented housing for such a long time, I really wanted my own place to settle down. A rental unit in which my daughter's family was living was also pretty small for them, so we wanted to build our own single-family home to live together. From the beginning, we let our son-in-law have part ownership of the joint house as a deal to live with us."*

The traditional custom of inheritance meant that home ownership of the family residence did not only mean owning a property, but also holding influential power over the younger generation. The family wealth of the older generation could be exchanged for family support from adult children in their old age. In modern society, however, with economic independence of older people and other critical factors (e.g. increased labour force participation by women), this reciprocity seemed less practiced. As a result, many older parents often remained as dominant providers of family support (usually financial) in family relations. In the case of coresidency, however, generational transfer of the household head seemed to occur naturally with a change of personal circumstances, such as older parents' retirement or widowhood, and to transform power relations between generations:

> At her retirement (when she was 60), N.H (70) purchased land next to their own house with her retirement allowance and expanded their property to twice the size. In the same year, her eldest son's family moved back from Yokohama in Greater Tokyo in order to live with their older parents. Her spouse died seven years later. *"Recently, since my coresident son was finally able to sell his own house in Yokohama, he decided to have our house rebuilt. The floor plan for a new home was all done by him and his wife. My friends often said to me why I didn't insist on getting my own kitchenette or other facilities in my living space, but I just followed my son's decision. These days I usually leave*

everything to them to decide, so I didn't voice my opinion regarding the new house. Also, when my old house was rebuilt by them, it was going to be theirs. That's why I let them do whatever they wanted to."

Social Status

Home ownership was also a symbol of obtaining social status for post-war families. Since keeping up public appearance was culturally and deeply rooted in older people's mentality, many of the older women had rather emotional reasons for owning their own house:

> K.H (73) and her spouse had their own home built before their daughter became independent. *"One of the reasons for having our own home built was that we wanted to marry off our daughter from our own home, not from rented housing or company housing."*

> N.T (74) lived in her own single-family home. She used to have a daughter, who died young. *"In the past, there was not such a place like a wedding hall. So, we, especially in the countryside where I come from, used to host a daughter's wedding banquet at home. That's why my husband and I had always been very enthusiastic about having our own house built big enough to host our daughter's wedding. We thought that we didn't need to be ashamed to invite our relatives all the way from our home town if we had our own house."*

Furthermore, for this generation, home ownership had been viewed as a rite of passage of younger people becoming a full adult. With the post-war expansion of nuclear family households combined with policy encouragement of home ownership, those newly formed families were expected to obtain their own place. The social expectation was created that 'everybody, which usually meant a male head of the nuclear households, was supposed to obtain his own home at some point of his life':

> O.M (78) lived with her eldest son and his family in her own single-family home. *"In the past, there used to be a saying that 'male adults had to [supposed to] build at least one house in their life time'. Since my husband had two houses built while he was alive, he was a lucky man."*

Creating Inequality through the Post-War Housing System

Process of Home Ownership

For some older people, home ownership was made possible through family wealth accumulated by their previous generations. Making a shift from company housing to home ownership was another common pathway for this cohort of older people in the post-war period. In Japan, the process of owning a house was commonly referred to as '*Ie wo tateru*' [building a house], which should be translated more accurately as 'having a house built'. Unlike Britain, where many houses last for well over a hundred years, the expected life-span of average houses in Japan is usually short, and the loss of houses by the Wars also accelerated housing needs for the generation, particularly in urban areas. Therefore, for this cohort of older people, becoming a home owner almost always meant having a new single-family home built, rather than purchasing an existing dwelling. The housing histories of those informants across three housing sectors illustrated the process of becoming or not becoming a home owner. An analysis of how the system created inequality in housing wealth among families and individuals in later life follows.

For some informants, family wealth was one of the paths to home ownership. Some of them sold their family assets (property) in rural areas, where their ancestors used to reside, as a means of having a modern house built in a more convenient, usually urban, location. Others had a new house built on their inherited land:

> K.H (73) and her spouse had their own house built to live with her nephew[1] and his family in the late 1960s. *"We had lived in company housing for years while my husband was being transferred around different cities. When my son got married, we needed our own house to live together. I sold some of the land which I inherited from my ancestor [through her parents] to raise funds. Then, we paid off all the debts – the cost of land and construction of housing – within five years. Because my husband was a salaried worker, we couldn't possibly think of arranging 20 to 30 year mortgages as young people do these days. When my daughter's family wanted to settle down a couple of years ago after having been transferred many times, I contributed half of the cost to purchase a house. She is going to inherit my assets anyway, so it doesn't make any difference if I give it to her now or later [except differences in inheritance tax]."*

O.M (78) lived in company housing for the first six years after the Second World War. *"I hated company housing. The security guards at the gate were always watching who went out wearing what kind of clothes, who brought back what, and so on. I often wished I could have climbed up the wall to get outside without passing the gate. That experience urged us to have our own home built. Luckily enough, my husband had land given to him by his parents, so we had our first house built there.... Twenty-one years later when we were forced to move because of a new highway plan, my relatives offered us the current land which was then a radish field. We had our second house built there."*

Due to Kitakyushu having been one of the major post-war industrial cities in Japan, many spouses of the informants were employed by relatively large companies with various occupational welfare schemes. One of the major benefits of occupational welfare was the provision of company housing. In reality, company housing benefited both the employees who were able to live in heavily subsidized rental houses, and the employers able to transfer their workers flexibly and frequently according to their needs. Many experienced several job-related moves while living in company housing:

When K.F (80)'s spouse retired from Nippon Steel, they had to find accommodation to move into. *"While he was employed with the company, we used to move around a lot within the city from one company house to another. When the year of his retirement came, we had to leave the company housing as soon as possible. The deadline was very strict. Since then, I've been living in the same rental housing for almost 30 years, and I'm going to stay here until I die."*

Many of those current home owners in the research lived in company housing during their spouse's employment. A downside of company housing was the restriction on eligibility. It was usually only available as long as they were employed by the company. The employees were, therefore, expected to find their own way out of company housing by the time they retired. Indeed, company housing commonly served as a stepping stone to home ownership:

M.S (77) and her spouse lived in company housing until his retirement. *"At my husband's retirement, we had a plan to buy a house with his retirement allowance. At that time, his company did not provide housing loans for their employees unlike these days. So, we had to wait till he received his retirement allowance. We found land in a newly*

> *developing residential town. His company was very generous to let us stay in the company house for another year until our house was built."*

T.S (77)'s spouse worked for Nippon Steel and they lived in company housing until they were in their early 50s. *"Because you had to leave company housing anyway at retirement, a common goal among salaried families in our generation was 'having your own house built by the time you retire'. Also, while raising children, and paying for their education and such, we had no spare money to put towards buying a house. So, it was quite common to have a house built after your children's independence, as we did."*

Within such a housing system, there were some unlucky people who could not get access to home ownership. Chapter 6 showed that being single, female, old and a renter could be the worst combination of factors. So, why were those people so disadvantaged in the Japanese housing system?

Non-Home Owners' Struggle

The fieldwork focused on interviewing older women and the meaning of 'single' has to be defined in that context. In the research, older women, who had been married and had families, but had become 'single' through either widowhood or divorce, were selected for interview, except two never-married women who had alternative means of family support. Evidently, marital status was one of the major indicators which determined women's access to home ownership, and thus their housing situation in later life. Differences in marital status were rather marked across the three welfare sectors. There was a clear demarcation line between home owners in the family and market sectors and non-owners in the state sector. Indeed, 'single' in this context does not mean women who had become widows in their old age, but ones such as those informants in the state sector who were either never married, or divorced or widowed much earlier in their marriage. Many older residents who ended up living in a public home, for example, had no family or came from dysfunctional families.[2]

For those women without a male principal worker in their households, their own irregular or informal employment situation was another reason for being unable to establish financial stability, and thus they experienced poorer housing situations in later life. Therefore, those single women were likely to end up being in the state sector housing. Without having proper or regular employment for themselves (or their spouse), most of the women in the state sector, for instance, had no access to occupational welfare, such as living in company housing, during their employment years:

> A.Y (71) had moved into a public home in early 1996. She had never married, and always lived with her older sister. *"My sister used to own three beauty salons and I helped her business living in one of them. She got divorced later on and moved to Kitakyushu where she started running a coffee shop. Again, I moved to live with her and helped her new business.... When she died last year, I was left with nothing, besides my own basic state pension. Since my sister was receiving a lot of money through her widow's pension, she had a lot of savings as well. But, my divorced niece as her only daughter legally inherited all her savings. The ownership of my sister's house in which we lived was transferred to my brother. At the time of my sister's death, my niece was also living with us. But, I wasn't comfortable living with her since she couldn't get hold of money and built up huge debts. I worried about myself becoming homeless if I stuck to her, so I went to a welfare office for help."*

> A.A (74) divorced her *youshi* husband a year after her marriage. Her only daughter died with cancer in 1990. She moved to a public home in 1993. *"After divorce, I had worked as an informal live-in housemaid for various families. I left my daughter with my own mother to take up the job. I moved around from one family to another.... When I started working for a private hospital, I was told that a parent and child should not have lived apart and there was a spare room for the two of us. We were finally able to live together [which did not last long because of my daughter's independence]. Even after I worked as a maid for more than 20 years, I tried to manage my life on my own in a rental apartment. But due to the expense of my daughter's medical treatment, I went on welfare after her death and later, moved to a public home."*

Those single women who could not get access to home ownership had to struggle on a low income in the small rental market or underdeveloped public housing sector. Those rental units which older women on low income could afford were usually in a much poorer condition than average rental housing, let alone owner-occupied housing. They were often cheaply built, poorly maintained, and likely to be beyond their expected life-span. In addition, security of tenure in such old rental stock was not assured so that those people living in such housing were always at risk of being removed. Many older women in the state sector had experienced eviction from typical old wooden apartment blocks before they moved into their current social housing:

> Since H.T (80) came to Kitakyushu at the age of 33, she had been forced to move seven times, mostly due to eviction (e.g. transfer of a building ownership, demolition of old apartment building). In 1974, she finally settled in public housing provided by the local authority. Last year, her public housing also became subject for demolition. She had priority to move into another newly-built public housing development with slightly increased rent. *"Because I receive my widow's pension, I was able to move into this new housing. Some pensioners in my previous housing had insufficient income to move into this new building. Inevitably, those people moved to another old public housing with much lower rents."*

> After having lived in private rental housing, A.A (74) moved into a public home. *"After my daughter died of cancer in 1990, I remained in a rental apartment for a while. But, the staff in the welfare office insisted that 'it was not safe to live alone, it was dangerous for an older person to live alone!' At first, I thought that I was still capable of living on my own. Then, I thought that being forgetful in old age, it was possible to do something careless such as starting fire in a kitchen. Also, because of such an old shabby apartment (the rent was only ¥15,000 [£75] per month), I started hearing a rumour that the apartment building would be demolished soon. So, I followed the social worker's advice and moved into this home."*

Since moving involves *costs*, it was not an easy option for low-income renters to move around according to their needs and preferences. Those women were either forced to move or chose to move, without sufficient financial means. Moving in old age was nothing more than a nuisance for those low-income renters:

> S.Y (74) experienced rent increases every two years in her rented single-family home. In order to secure her accommodation with her own small pension and savings, she moved into public housing provided by the Housing Corporation in the late 1970s. At that time, she had to apply jointly with her nephew to meet the eligibility criteria of the project. *"Now, I live on the second floor of a four-storey building without an elevator. The local authority these days has a new policy to allow us, older people, to move down to a ground floor unit of the same building [subject to the availability], which is supposed to provide us with greater accessibility and more convenience. But, you know, when you*

want to move, even to downstairs, it costs a lot to pay somebody to move your stuff and refurbish the previous accommodation [usually, tenants are obliged to refurbish a rental unit before they move out]. I have no money to do that."

If you rely on the 'risk-averse' rental housing market, problems begin to appear when they reach a certain age. Entry to rental housing in old age seems almost impossible in Japan. Becoming a renter or trying to look for another private rental housing in old age poses a great challenge, especially for single women:

> A.A (72) was a 60-year-old home owner when her spouse died. *"I experienced a nightmare. After I became a widow, my sisters suggested I rent an apartment near their houses. 'Since you have sufficient pension funds, you can pay your rent and still have enough money to live on', they said. One of my sisters went ahead and tried to find an apartment unit for me. Even though I was still in my mid-60s, I was rejected by every single estate agency which she contacted. The agents said, 'we don't rent an apartment to "single" women, especially women over 65'. Even though my four sisters insisted on becoming guarantors for me, it wasn't any help. When renting housing, there is no chance for 'single' older women, because we are considered to be a potential problem. That's part of the reason why I bought the life-estate of this private retirement flat."*

Recently, these issues have become more recognized and an area of concern for younger single women. A new market trend showed that single women in their 30s and 40s have started purchasing a condominium in urban areas (*Asahi Shinbun*, evening 7 April 1997, p. 1). Younger women's economic independence gained through their increased labour force participation, and resulting postponement of marriage, can be factors accelerating this phenomenon. Financial dependency on a spouse by marriage seems no longer to be a single viable option for those 'career' women seeking to secure their housing.

How to Make Residential Choices

The second major objective of this chapter is to analyse how these older women made their residential choices, and what criteria those choices were based on. Older people's views on family relations, including the traditional practice of coresidency, were closely examined in Chapter 2, and this chapter focuses particularly on reasons for the recent increase of elderly-only households.   The older women in the research pointed to many important factors in their residential choices, such as established social networks and maintaining freedom.   The research revealed that older women's preferences were moving towards a higher demand for independent living.

Social Networks in a Familiar Neighbourhood

Social networks in a familiar neighbourhood were considered to be a major factor in older women's residential choices.   The older women who had strong and sufficient social networks were more embedded in a community, and thus tended to remain living independently from their adult children, compared with others whose prominent ties lay within the family.   There appeared to be a link between their residential choices and the degree of social ties:

> S.F (74) lived across the street from her first son's house.   Her relationship with his family stayed quite formal and dry, since her visits to his house were limited for ritual purposes (praying twice a day to their ancestor's memorial table).   Otherwise, they did not do anything together, such as having meals.   Instead, she enjoyed taking out ready-made *sushi* and lunch boxes on her own.   *"I feel much closer to my older neighbours including old customers of my store which we used to run [than my son's family].   If we don't see each other for a while, we ask after each other's health.   They are much easier to talk to and much quicker to understand me than, my daughter-in-law, for example.   I have no intention of moving into my son's house."*

> O.T (71) lived in her single-family home with her unmarried daughter (46).   She could not even think of moving out from her community in which she had plenty of friends of her own age and many social activities.   *"When I need old age care in the future, I would rather go to the nearest hospital than another daughter's house in Tokyo.   In the nearest hospital, my friends would be often able to visit me.   My coresident daughter wants to sell this old single-family home and move to a condominium in a better location.   But, she can do so after I die."*

In contemporary society, increased geographic mobility of the younger generations has tended to create a physical separation between older parents and adult children. As a result, older parents were likely to be placed in a position that they had to choose between family support in coresidency and social ties in a familiar neighbourhood. In such circumstances, starting coresidency in later life sometimes broke down existing social networks. Many older women in the research expressed their preference for remaining in their neighbourhood as long as possible with friends of their own age, rather than moving to an unfamiliar place where they could only associate with their coresident family:

> One year after M.H (80)'s spouse's death, she moved a long distance to live near her son's family. Moving into a private purpose-built retirement flat was a very attractive option for her since it provided safety and security, three hot meals a day, and a social life. She enjoyed living with people of her own age, and attending various social clubs including her favourite tea ceremony class in the housing development. After two years, when she had established her social circle in the development, her son was again transferred to the Tokyo region. *"I was wondering what to do if I was asked to go with his family [to his next posting]. My son told me that I was welcome to come with them, but a house in the suburb would be less convenient than here. Because they were going to live in company housing, it wouldn't have a big common bath, and only young families would be living there. I also thought that in such an environment, it would be hard to meet older people I could befriend. So, I decided to stay put in this housing. Actually, I'd already made up my mind a long ago."*

> M.S (77) had once moved a long distance with her sick spouse to live with their son and his family. At that time, she desperately needed some family support to care for her spouse who had cancer. *"My husband had always wished to live with our son. But, when we were about to move, he didn't want to go, and cried in front of his friends in old-folks club. We moved, anyway.... A couple of months later when my husband died, I started feeling very lonely. There was not much conversation with my son's wife, and I couldn't make new friends in the new town, either. I decided to move back here and live independently at home in our neighbourhood. My son still insists that I move back in his house, but I don't think so. Now, I understand older people [my husband]'s feeling – He didn't want to live away from his familiar people and place. Now, I regret that I made him go."*

In post-war society, however, *chi-en* [blood relations] and *chi-en* [community ties][3] are less emphasized. High occupational related mobility made the society less static and consequently harder to establish strong community-based family ties. To some extent, those ties were replaced by a different type of ties, called *sha-en* [company based ties], especially for employees.

Freedom from the Husband-Wife Relationship

According to family tradition, older women used to follow their spouse's decisions, and form a social circle based on a husband-wife relationship. After their spouse's death, therefore, many of those widows in the research experienced a major life change, often for the better. Many women explained how much and how positively their social circle and life improved. Some of them also began to find and enjoy their own independence in widowhood. Consequently, the freedom led the women to choose independent living with their social ties rather than to rely entirely on their adult children. In this situation, moving out of the community was not a desirable option, since family ties could carry on at a distance but strong community ties only exist living in a community:

> T.S (77)'s independent living in her single-family home was supported by social networks which she established after her spouse's death. *"While my husband was alive, he did all community related work on his own. I didn't get involved in anything at all, but stayed at home sewing. After he died, I'm basically out all the time – going to older people's community club and related activities. I surprised myself how much my personality and lifestyle have changed. I enjoy going out to meet people in the community, and like living in this neighbourhood. I suppose that I'll have to move into my son's house sooner or later, but it's too far from here. I think that another two to three years are OK* (to be on my own). *When my grandchildren become independent, my youngest daughter will be less burdened to take care of them. Maybe, that's the time to start living with them. Perhaps, I'll remain here until I really become bed-ridden, and then be sent to hospital.... Ummm, before that, I don't really want to leave this house."*

At their retirement, A.A (72)'s spouse decided to purchase a house and move from Tokyo to his home town. *"Because I was married to him, I had no say in his decision but used to follow him. In our generation, it was said that 'onna wa sankai ni Ie nasi' [once women were married, there was no other home to go back to but their husband's]."* She was ready to follow him wherever he wanted to go, even though she had no relation to the people and the place of his home town. He died two years after they moved to his home town, but she remained there. On the seventh anniversary after his death, she finally felt that she was able to make her own decision. She moved into a private purpose-built retirement flat, located close enough to visit his grave once a month, instead of moving closer to her relatives' houses or coresiding with her son's family.

O.M (78)'s spouse died a year ago. *"Wherever I went out to enjoy myself, I used to leave there early to come home and look after my sick husband. I used to envy those widow friends who had completed their duties. Finally, I'm part of the widow group. Now, I joined the ranks. My husband wouldn't be angry if I started enjoying myself. I had done as much as I could do for him."*

K.H (73) had not liked going out with her spouse while he was alive. He did not allow her to go out often with her friends, either. *"When he died, I thought that my life was going to bloom from now on! It's going to be my second spring time of life. My friends warned me to remain quiet and mourn for a little longer, but I couldn't. I could not enjoy my youth because of the Wars. Now, I don't need to consult with anybody anymore. I can do whatever I want to. These days, I do lots of traveling, even overseas, and attend continuing education classes."*

U.Y (70) had been working as a nursery teacher, and after retirement, as a volunteer for a telephone life-line. She lived independently in her own single-family home. *"When my husband retired, we also decided to retire from our marriage, become just house mates, and do whatever each of us wanted to do individually. The reason behind this was that I wanted to prepare for independent living when one of us became widowed in the future."*

Social Services and Economic Independence

Economic independence of older people, combined with the development of social service delivery as an alternative means to family support, was a major practical reason for expanding older people's opportunities and choices for independent living. The necessity of coresidency as a venue to provide old age care in the family was reduced to a great degree in modern society. A substantial improvement of social services, both in the public and the market areas, was still needed to support those older people's independent living:

U.Y (70) preferred remaining independently in her own single-family home located close to her sisters' houses, to moving to Tokyo in order to live with her son's family. *"For many older parents, the main reason for living with adult children could be receiving old age care in the future. Since young people these days are more business-like and do things for you if you pay, I set aside some money for whoever would take care of me when I become bed-ridden. I've never thought about moving into my children's house. I don't mind being cared for by non-relatives."*

On the other hand, underdeveloped social services prevented some older women, who needed assistance but could not or did not want to rely on their adult children, from independent living or choosing a staying-put option. Unnecessary institutionalization of older people sometimes occurred due to such an underdeveloped system. Many home residents, especially women, were still capable of living in ordinary housing, if more adequate and affordable housing with social service delivery were available:

N.M (75) moved to a public home in the late 1980s. After she divorced her *youshi* spouse at 57, she managed her own life working part-time in a restaurant kitchen, and living in private rental housing. Five years later, she fell down the stairs in her apartment, and stayed in hospital for two months with a broken hip. The accident took her job and means of support away from her, so she went on welfare (public assistance for living protection). *"After I was back from hospital, my daughter-in-law [her only son's wife] used to come to my apartment and help me with my laundry and cleaning. Since my son's family lived near my apartment, she visited me every day very early in the morning to do the domestic work for me. If I didn't have children, or they lived far away from me, or were not willing to give me their hand, I couldn't have lived independently for those years after the accident. When I reached 65 and started receiving a tiny pension, staff in the welfare office recommended to move into a home."*

After her spouse's death, H.S (77) already on welfare moved to live close to her daughter's family. She had lived with them for six months until conflicts between the generations became obvious. When she needed a place to live independently, social housing located in a very isolated and inconvenient place was the only house which she could afford. Since the two-storey apartment was old and not well designed for single older females, she only used the ground floor. Also, it was difficult for her to manage her life without support services. Once she got hospitalized with a minor knee problem, she found that even sharing a dingy hospital ward with other patients was much better than living alone in her apartment *"If I can choose [between going back to live in her social housing and staying put in hospital], I would like to stay in hospital as long as possible [even without any critical condition]."*

Human Contacts in Group Living

If older people want to remain independent from their adult children, and at the same time, enjoy the privilege of being in a supportive environment, group living offers as an attractive option. It provides older residents with many advantages such as friendship and social interaction with people in their age group, as well as safety, security and other social services. In such living environments, some older women who had been isolated from their family and society have achieved a higher degree of interaction with other people. Some informants explained how their living situation improved after moving into a group home, and others expressed their preference for living with other people if possible:

S.Y (74) lived independently in a rental unit provided by the Housing Corporation. She had two widowed sisters. One of the sisters suggested an idea that the three of them live together. *"Because we are blood-related, we could be selfish to each other and possibly always demand what 'I' want. So, if I have a choice, I'd rather live with friends or other older people than those sisters. I can be more patient with other people.... The ideal housing for me is a group home for older people. It is easy for me to communicate with people of my own age. Through my brother-in-law, I asked a welfare office about my financial capability to move into a group home [public home for relatively healthy older people]. Although it was possible with my meager pension, the waiting list was too long."*

When K.H (79)'s coresidency with her youngest son's family broke down and she started living alone in a rental apartment, she found independent living to be a lonely experience. Because her wooden apartment building was very old and without a bathroom, only three out of six units in the building were occupied. That was the only apartment which her four children together could afford to rent for her (each paid ¥5,000 [£25] per month). *"At first, I thought that it was wonderful to live alone without worrying about other people. Then, soon, I started feeling very lonely. I sometimes went to take a bath in my nearby daughter's house, but of course, I couldn't go there every day. There was no one around to speak to, no older people living near-by, and the only person always there was an unemployed guy upstairs. I often ended the day without speaking to anyone."* After four months of independent living, she requested to move into a public home at the local welfare office. *"My image of 'old folk's home' was a place where old men and women live quietly sitting without doing anything. Actually, there are so many social activities and clubs such as gateball, flower arrangements, and singing folk songs going on in a home. I was so lucky to be able to move into this home. It's such fun to chat with other residents."*

A.A (72) had been living in a private purpose-built retirement flat for five years. *"I had remained in my husband's home town for seven more years after his death. When I decided to move, I thought that since I didn't have my own family anymore [she considered her spouse to be her family not her married adult children], it was better to move to somewhere I could make many friends of my own age. That's why I chose this housing."*

Apart from public homes, group living for older people is a relatively new concept in Japan. The use of and demand for group homes for relatively healthy older people are developing. Currently, such homes are mainly available in two very different forms – highly subsidized public homes which are still targeted on people below the poverty line; and luxury private developments in the market, planned and built during the period of the bubble economy in the late 1980s. There are not many group homes which serve middle-income older people:

O.T (71) was a single-family home owner widowed after her spouse's death. Because of his early death, she struggled as a young widow to raise her three children. *"Now, my children are also managing their lives with all their might. I don't think that I should move into their tiny condominiums in Tokyo and cause them trouble. I'd rather move into a nursing home. If the waiting list for public housing is too long, I wouldn't mind paying ¥100,000 to ¥150,000 [£500 to £750] per month to live in a private housing for older people. In a group home, I can keep enjoying my hobby – singing karaoke and dancing with other residents."*

Other women like O.T (71) were 'asset-rich but cash-poor'; in other words, despite owning their own home, the expectations of their adult children prevented them from selling their property to raise funds. This situation did not allow such women to purchase a unit in the luxury private housing development, and also made them ineligible for existing group housing options.

Privacy and Freedom in a New Form of Intergenerational Living

Interaction with other age groups through coresidency was in many ways still desired by older women. As mentioned in Chapter 6, the problem of lacking privacy, freedom and independence in the traditional form of shared arrangement has been reduced through the introduction of two-household accommodation. When this ideal form of housing becomes more economically viable, it is likely to improve the current situation of older women in coresidency. It may also encourage renewed interest in coresidency:

> N.T (74) lived in her single-family home with her son's family. After her spouse's death, the younger family moved into her house. Although she shared all facilities such as a kitchen and a bathroom, she basically lived her own life in her tiny space (a six *tatami*-mat room)[4] separately from her coresident son's family. Unless her son's wife cooked special meals for the whole family, the two generations usually cooked separately. She cooked for herself and brought food in her own room to eat. Her small room was equipped with a refrigerator, a cupboard and a TV. Since she did not like to negotiate for space or push her demands forward, she always let her son's wife have priority. In order to gain her own space and freedom, she wished to live in a two-household house. *"My friends always hesitate to visit me because of my coresident daughter-in-law. I really want my own entrance to my room, then my friends can visit me freely without meeting my daughter-in-law. Our generation is very much reserved and careful about not disturbing other people. The younger generation, on the other hand, don't have such reservations. So, my daughter-in-law's friends and relatives come anytime without thinking about me, and take over the whole space without the slightest hesitation. I never thought about this problem when we built this house – now, this house is not big enough to convert into two-household housing."*

For many people like N.T (74), it is an unrealistic dream to purchase a large piece of land to build two-household housing, or to have sufficient financial means to build such a costly new house on existing land in later life.

Consequently, many of the older women suggested a more feasible and desirable option; living nearby their adult children, especially their daughter's family:

> T.S (77) lived independently in her own house near her youngest daughter's house. *"It's not good [older parents and adult children] to be together. If you live together, you end up fighting. I think that the saying, 'it's better to live "supu no samenai kyori" [a distance which soup does not get cold to bring] from your adult children', is true. I'd like to live independently as long as possible near my daughter's house while I'm living in good health."*

Concluding Comments

Despite family tradition and constraints, a growing number of older women have started making their own choices of residential living in later life. To a certain extent, an expansion of elderly-only households and the decreasing rates of coresidency in contemporary society reflects older women's growing preferences for independent living from their adult children. Why do those older women prefer to live independently? The explanations for this recent trend include a combination of factors: the increased labour force participation by women; the increased (higher education or job-related) geographic mobility of younger people; greater economic independence of older people (with their own savings and pensions); and also the inadequate size and quality of housing to enable coresidency in urban areas. However, the main reason for the increasing separation of older parents and adult children seems largely due to people's changing views of life and family over generations. Living independently allows older people to avoid unnecessary conflicts with younger generations, to enhance the importance of their individual life and pursuits, and also to maximize freedom and privacy in their residential setting.

There is another view which suggests that the recent phenomenon is a temporary separation until those older people really need assistance from their adult children. For various reasons, many women in the research who lived independently from their children were, however, reluctant to live together with their children even after their personal circumstances change. Women, particularly in especially-equipped housing for older people, such as public homes and private developments, tended to see their current housing as a home for the rest of their life. Even those who were at risk of becoming dependent in their own single-family home expressed a preference to remain independent of their children, and to move to hospital if they became bed-ridden. Overall, the research revealed that a more substantial change towards independent living had been occurring in older people's residential choices.

Notes

1   She and her spouse adopted their nephew when he was orphaned. She often referred to her nephew as her son.
2   Interview with a manager of a public home for older people.
3   Different Chinese characters represent these two concepts, pronunced in the same way.
4   6 *tatami*-mat is equivalent to 9.72 m².

8   Conclusions

Conceptual Findings

This book set out to explore the experiences of older women in post-war Japanese society, through the lens of family and housing histories of older Japanese women. Three broad themes – *family relations, welfare systems,* and *housing* – were chosen to highlight issues surrounding the changing role and position of women in the family and society.

First, the evolution of the Japanese family in the post-war period was examined. One of the major transformations was in their household structures – from the traditional extended family to various other forms and more individualistic arrangements as characterized by increasing numbers of nuclear households, particularly elderly-only households. In addition, the study revealed that family traditions have also been transformed. Post-war socio-economic and legal changes inevitably introduced new ideologies, functions and changed relationships within the family. The authority which older parents used to hold over their children has been eroded with the abolition of the *Ie* system. As a result, apart from the unique *giri* relationship, women have been liberated from traditional roles and positions in the family. Modernization and industrialization have also played their part in separating older parents from their adult children, both geographically and functionally. Social change (e.g. paid work for married women, increased financial commitments for a younger couple, such as their children's education and mortgages) presented competing tasks for younger people, and raised the economic independence of older parents (e.g. through pension and savings). For many of the women, therefore, receiving care in their old age was viewed as a burden on their children rather than as a means of support that they could naturally expect. As a consequence, the expectations and the actual practice of older people of living with their adult children (and receiving support from them) have declined significantly. Increasing numbers of older people in urban areas have started making positive choices concerning their housing (and living arrangements) in later life.

Second, the book discussed the origin, structure and the development process of the post-war welfare system in Japan. Throughout this period, Japan developed a residual welfare model with a larger role played by the market (welfare industry) and enterprises (providing occupational welfare for their employees), while the family continued to provide substantial welfare to other members. However, considering social change, the current economic crisis, and the rapidly ageing society, the current approach is coming under strain. The capacity of the family as a welfare provider is eroding with changing family values and household structures. The new global economy and the post-bubble recession are causing the breakdown of the conventional employment system, and thus a review of the provision of occupational welfare is essential. As a result, a model similar to the American model of a 'liberal-residual' welfare state is being adopted. Welfare services will be no longer granted freely or universally by the state, the traditional family, or employers, but instead will increasingly become more market-oriented and based on a contract between users and various welfare providers. In Japan, where the emphasis on direct state intervention was originally minimal, the above shift currently taking place is creating a new scenario for the welfare state into the twenty-first century.

The development of the post-war social system and labour market in Japan created gender inequalities and wealth gaps among individuals and families. The male breadwinner family model reinforced gender roles in married couples by sustaining unpaid female domestic workers, and thus causing many women to become financially dependent on their spouses. As a result, the post-war labour market became male-dominated, with women's access to paid work and employment status restricted. Combined with the employment mechanism being predominantly 'large-firm oriented', the system created wealth gaps among families according to the employment of the principal worker of the household. In addition, social security systems based on 'the family as a unit' accentuated the relative poverty of older single women. It was evident that for those women outside a conventional family structure, the system placed them at a considerable disadvantage. There were many difficulties facing single women (or female-headed households) which prevented them from benefiting fully from the system and establishing a means for independent living in their old age.

The above issues have influenced the housing destinations of Japanese people in their later years. Due to the post-war emphasis on home ownership, housing options for Japanese people have been very limited. For example, moving into more suitable housing in old age posed a great challenge for older people due to limited public provision, costly alternatives in the market, and the discrimination of property owners towards older renters. The economic disadvantages of single women (and female-headed households) in society also restricted their access to quality housing, including home ownership. The research found that being female and single as well as a renter represented probably the worst combination of factors in housing for later life.

Overall, social change in the rapidly ageing society has created greater demand for new types of housing and services for older people. The research has highlighted that either through choice or constraint, traditional extended family living has shifted towards more individualistic housing alternatives for older people in urban areas. The problem of maintaining privacy, freedom, and independence in traditional shared living has become accentuated in modern society. Two-household housing was mentioned by some of the women as one of the ideal housing alternatives. With new ways of living added to traditional ones, it presented the possibility of coresidency, thus enhancing the ability of older people to maintain their independence with younger people, while allowing more privacy and independence at home and in the community. For many people, however, it is an unrealistic dream to have such housing built in later life. Living only a short distance from their adult children, especially from daughters, was seen by some as a more realistic and desirable aspiration. Living independently for as long as possible without becoming a burden to their adult children was, indeed, the collective wish among many of the older women.

Policy Analysis

In Japan, the post-war miracle of economic growth has been often contrasted with the unbalanced growth of public sector welfare, especially the provision of housing and social services. Additionally, criticism has been levelled at the protected nature of the Japanese economy, characterized by its comprehensive rules and regulations (e.g. the rice market, the financial sector). In recent years, however, the nation's growth has required economic openness which, in turn, has entailed tougher competition and greater vulnerability to international trade, finance and capital movements (Esping-Andersen, 1996). Outside pressure has inevitably forced Japan to deregulate its economy and to review its social policies in line with international trends.

Since the economic 'bubble' burst in the early 1990s, the Japanese economy has lost its momentum, having entered its worst recession since the Second World War. The ageing of Japanese society is also increasingly becoming a serious issue, upsetting the balance between the working and dependant population. All these factors necessitate a review of current socio-economic systems and a reappraisal of issues affecting the nation's public resources. Future policy options, especially those of housing and welfare, will be impacted upon by the new global economy and the current economic crisis in Japan.

First, we have recently witnessed how a more open economy and the current recession are helping to transform the unique practice of Japanese employment, known as 'Japanese-style management'. With globalization and accompanying deregulation, Japanese corporations have to seek creative (alternative) ways of cutting costs and achieving greater productivity in order to compete and survive in both domestic and international markets. Some corporations have, therefore, begun to question their conventional 'firm-as-a-family' model, adopting more contractual, individualistic and competitive arrangements in areas such as hiring practices, salary structures and occupational benefits (http://www.jinjapan.org/insight/html, 28 May 1998). As a result, the percentage of workers on full occupational benefits has fallen since the mid-1990s. Instead, flexible workers, such as part-time workers and contract workers have been increasing to meet the changing needs of the corporations. The breakdown of the conventional employment system illustrates how individuals and families will have to insure themselves in the market and society without the security previously offered by employment and occupational welfare schemes. Among those benefits, the provision of company housing has also been in decline.

Second, how has housing policy and the housing market been responding to these transformations? Post-war housing provision in Japan has largely been driven by the private sector, with the assistance of corporations. During the period of post-war economic growth, company housing served as a stepping stone for many workers (and their families) to home ownership. With the transformation of the management system in many corporations, the direction of company housing seems to be following a path similar to that of post-war housing policy. The direct provision of company housing has been gradually replaced with indirect housing assistance, such as housing loans, saving programs, and rent subsidies. With a reduction of company housing, the issue of home ownership is likely to continue to dominate the Japanese housing scene over the twenty-first century. One change observed in the ownership sector is that of dwelling type. Considering the urban congestion and the high land prices, the previously favoured option of owning a single-family home has been replaced, both in terms of popularity and practicality, by purchasing a condominium, particularly in inner cities. This shift is likely to impact upon conventional housing practices of older people. Compared with an average single-family home, the smaller unit size of condominiums is likely to discourage intergenerational living, resulting in less support exchange in coresidency. Moreover, since the resale value of condominiums tends to drop significantly over time, home ownership may not remain as a strong means of wealth accumulation. If selling such a unit in later life does not fund their move to supportive housing for older people, owning a condominium may restrict people's residential mobility.

Attempts by various governments to provide increased numbers of housing developments for older people (including those in the public-private partnership) have already run into difficulties as a result of a change in Japan's economic fortunes. Not only is housing for older people in short supply, but there is also unlikely to be significant expansion in public sector rental units. With a proposed legal amendment to leasehold agreements, the situation of individual renters and the future of the rental sector as a whole will remain uncertain. One optimistic assumption of the deregulation is an expansion of larger rental stocks, currently under-utilized, to house families. The increased flexibility of property owners, granted by the proposed 'Short-Term Leasehold Act' in 1998, however, may result in instability for many renters by reducing their security of tenure. Additionally, eviction may become a serious threat for those renters who occupy older dwellings, since the deregulation may accelerate urban redevelopment. Without further public assistance such as rent subsidies, the cost of any transfer is likely to fall on the low-income renters themselves. In Japan, a renter-friendly housing market seems unlikely in the near future.

Third, what is the future of social services for older people under the current direction of the government? The rapidly ageing society poses great challenges, particularly for some areas of social policy, since both an increase in the number of bed-ridden older people, and those suffering from dementia, is predicted. Due to increased longevity, family carers have also been ageing, and periods of care have often become prolonged. Additionally, many other factors such as increased labour force participation by women, changing family traditions, and increasing numbers of elderly-only households have been eroding both the capacity for family support and the willingness of family members to carry it out. In response, it has become a primary need to establish a social support system to enable people to spend their later life independently, even if they require substantial support such as nursing care. The promotion of community care schemes can be viewed, therefore, as a more cost-effective and universal solution than the development of further institutional housing.

Such community care schemes need to be developed hand-in-hand with substantial improvements in the support facilities and services available for older people. Some local authorities have already started funding housing adaptation programs in order to prevent older people from unnecessary institutionalization. Moreover, because of the increasing cost burden of the ageing society, the national government has been reforming the current social security system through the introduction of 'public insurance for nursing care'. A few months before the planned April 2000 start of the scheme, the government was forced to reconsider the original plan. The plan was criticized for asking the nation (including low-income older people themselves) to contribute to the scheme without securing the provision of essential services. Considering the decline in family resources, one of the major problems holding back widespread promotion of this new scheme appears to be the shortage of care providers (Ueno, *Asahi Shinbun*, 22 December 1997, p. 4). It is crucial to effectively organize the potential human resources in such a labour-short Japanese economy, especially in such a service-intensive industry. Japan will face the same problems as other mature welfare states such as Sweden. In those countries, the welfare services are provided by foreign workers from neighbouring countries, due to the poor working conditions and low wages for care service providers. Besides the interest expressed in the private sector regarding the 'silver' industry, the role of non-profit organizations (e.g. citizen's organizations, women's groups, co-ops) has been recently recognized as a potential growth area. When these organizations become eligible to tender for local authority welfare schemes, it is likely to become the most cost-effective option for older people, considering the current cost performance of the public and private services. Since the majority of potential care workers both in the private and voluntary sectors are women, however, it is controversial as to whether the creation of such a service industry will reinforce the gender-biased labour market. It will also be necessary to develop a system to monitor both the quality of services and the working conditions of service providers.

Finally, apart from permitting open market and free labour movement, globalization must also allow social security systems to develop to support such practices. For example, the development of an 'international pension scheme', including open contributions and benefits across nations, is a case in point (Miyajima, 1997). It is not uncommon these days for Japanese employees to spend several years working abroad. About 118,000 employees of Japanese corporations were based in foreign countries in 1994 (Ministry of Foreign Affairs, 1995). These workers usually continue to contribute to Japanese occupational pension schemes in order to receive the maximum benefits (based on the contribution years) at retirement. The problem of 'double-burden' occurs if a country in which these people work also require compulsory contributions to be made to separate pension schemes. The development of an international pension scheme based on an agreement between two countries is likely to reduce the financial burden of the cross-national workforce, and allow more flexible but secure employment patterns in the new global economy.

Bibliography

Abe, Y., Iwata, K., Segawa, N., Nomura, T. and Yoshida, K. (1997), '*Teiki Shakuya-Ken Ron wo Megutte* [The Theory of Periodical Tenancy Rights]', *Jurist*, No. 1124: pp. 4-40.

Ageing Sogo Kenkyu Centre. (1995), '*21 Seiki heno Kuni no Shisaku* [National Policy Toward Twenty-First Century]', *Aging*, Summer: pp. 2-17.

Anderson, S.J. (1992), 'The Policy Process and Social Policy in Japan', *PS: Political Science & Politics*, March: pp. 36-43.

Anderson, S.J. (1993), *Welfare Policy and Politics in Japan: Beyond the Developmental State*, New York: Paragon House.

Benedict, R. (1947), *The Chrysanthemum and the Sword: Patterns of Japanese Culture*, London: Secker & Warburg.

Berggren, C. and Nomura, M. (1997), *The Resilience of Corporate Japan: New Competitive Strategies and Personnel Practices*, London: Paul Chapman Publishing.

Blank, T.O. (1988), *Older Persons and Their Housing: Today and Tomorrow*, Springfield: Charles C. Thomas Publisher.

Borthwick, M. (1992), *Pacific Century: The Emergence of Modern Pacific Asia*, Boulder: Westview.

Campbell, J.C. (1992), *How Policies Change: The Japanese Government and the Aging Society*, Princeton: Princeton University Press.

Chellis, R.D.,Seagle, Jr., J.F. and Seagle, B.M. (1982), *Congregate Housing for Older People: A Solution for the 1980s*, Toronto: Lexington Books.

City of Kitakyushu, Japan. (1992), *Kourei-sha Jittai Chousa [Survey on the Situations of Older People]*, Kitakyushu.

City of Kitakyushu, Japan. (1994), *Kitakyushu-shi Kourei-ka Shakai Taisaku Sougou Keikaku: Dai Ichi-ji Jisshi Keikaku [Master Plan for Ageing Society in Kitakyushu]*, Kitakyushu.

Clark, R. (1979), *The Japanese Company*, New Haven: Yale University Press.

Cochrane, A. (1993), 'Comparative Approaches and Social Policy', in A. Cochrane and J. Clarke (ed), *Comparing Welfare States: Britain in International Context*, London: Sage.

Coleman, D. and Salt, J. (1992), *The British Population: Patterns, Trends, and Processes*, Oxford: Oxford University Press.

Cowgill, D. (1974), 'Aging and Modernization: A Revision of the Theory', in J.F. Gubrium (ed), *Late Life*, Springfield, IL: Thomas.

Cowgill, D. (1986), *Aging Around the World*, Belmont, CA: Wadsworth.

Cowgill, D and Holmes, L. (eds) (1972), *Aging and Modernization*, New York: Appleton-Century-Crofts.

Das, M.S. and Bardis, P.D. (1978), 'Editors' Introduction', in M.S. Das and P.D. Bardis (eds), *The Family in Asia*, New Delhi: Vikas Publishing House.

Davis, K. and van den Oever, P. (1981), 'Age Relations and Public Policy in Advanced Societies', *Population and Development Review*, 7 (1): pp. 1-18.

Dictionary of Human Geography, The. (3rd Edition) (1994), R.J. Johnston, D. Gregory and D.M. Smith (eds), Oxford: Blackwell.

Dore, R. (1973), *British Factory – Japanese Factory*, Berkeley: University of California Press.

Dore, R. (1987), *Taking Japan Seriously: A Confucian Perspective on Leading Economic Issues*, London: Athlone Press.

Dupuis, A. and Thorns, D.C. (1996), 'Meanings of Home for Older Home Owners', *Housing Studies*, Vol. 11, No. 4: pp. 485-501.

Economic Planning Agency, Japan. (1982), *Annual Report on National Life 1981*, Tokyo: Ministry of Finance Printing Bureau.

Esping-Andersen, G. (1990), *The Three Worlds of Welfare Capitalism*, Cambridge: Polity Press.

Esping-Andersen, G. (1993), 'Post-Industrial Class Structures: An Analytical Framework', in G. Esping-Andersen (ed), *Changing Classes: Stratification and Mobility in Post-Industrial Societies*, London: Sage.

Esping-Andersen, G. (1996), 'Conclusion: Positive-Sum Solutions in a World of Trade-Offs?', in G. Esping-Andersen (ed), *Welfare States in Transition: National Adaptations in Global Economies*, London: Sage.

Esping-Andersen, G. (1997), 'Hybrid or Unique?: The Japanese Welfare State Between Europe and America', *Journal of European Social Policy*, 7 (3): pp. 179-89.

Evers, A. (1993), 'The Welfare Mix Approach: Understanding the Pluralism of Welfare Systems', in A. Evers and I. Svetlik (eds), *Balancing Pluralism: New Welfare Mixes in Care for the Elderly*, Aldershot: Avebury.

Finch, J. (1989), *Family Obligations and Social Change*, Cambridge: Polity Press.

Finch, J. (1993), "It's Great to Have Someone to Talk to': Ethics and Politics of Interviewing Women', in M. Hammersley (ed), *Social Research: Philosophy, Politics and Practice*, London: Sage.

Forrest, R. and Murie, A (eds). (1995), *Housing and Family Wealth: Comparative International Perspectives*, London: Routledge.

Fujita, Y. (1984), *Employee Benefits and Industrial Relations*, Tokyo: Japan Institute of Labour.

Garcia, C. (1993), 'What do We Mean by Extended Family? A Closer Look at Hispanic Multigenerational Families', *Journal of Cross-Cultural Gerontology*, 8: pp. 137-46.

Gibson, M. J. (1992), 'Public Health and Social Policy', in H. Kendig, A. Hashimoto and L.C. Coppard (eds), *Family Support for the Elderly: The International Experience*, Oxford: Oxford University Press.

Giele, J.Z. (1982), 'Family and Social Network', in R.H. Binstock, W.S Chow and J.H. Schulz (eds), *International Perspectives on Aging: Population and Policy Challenges*, New York: United Nations Fund for Population Activities.

Golant, S.M. (1992), *Housing America's Elderly: Many Possibilities / Few Choices*, Newbury Park: Sage.

Goode, W.J. (1963), *World Revolution and Family Patterns*, New York: Free Press.

Goodman, R. and Peng, I. (1996), 'The East Asian Welfare States: Peripatetic Learning, Adaptive Change, and Nation-Building', in G. Esping-Andersen (ed), *Welfare States in Transition: National Adaptations in Global Economies*, London: Sage.

Gould, A. (1993), *Capitalist Welfare Systems: A Comparison of Japan, Britain and Sweden*, London: Longman.

Granger, B. and Kaye, L.W. (1991), 'Assessing Consumer Need and Demand for Service-Assisted Housing in Pennsylvania', in L. Kaye and A. Monk (ed), *Congregate Housing for the Elderly: Theoretical, Policy and Programmatic Perspectives*, Binghamton: Haworth Press.

Hall, R. (1988), *Enterprise Welfare in Japan: Its Development and Role*, Discussion Paper, Suntory-Toyota International Centre for Economics and Related Disciplines, June.

Harada, S. (1998), '*Teiki Shakka Ken Dounyuu-Ron no Nerai ha Nanika* [What is the Purpose of Introducing Short-Term Leasehold]', *Sekai*, February: pp. 22-6.

Harada, T. (1987), '*Kazoku Keitai no Hendou* [Changing Family Formation]', *Nihon no Shakai-gaku 4 Gendai Kazoku [Sociology of Japan 4 Contemporary Family]*, Tokyo: Tokyo University Press.

Hareven, T.K. (1982), *Family Time and Industrial Time*, New York: Cambridge University Press.

Hareven, T.K. (1994), 'Family Change and Historical Change', in M.W. Riley, R.L. Kahn and A. Foner (eds), *Age and Structural Lag: Society's Failure to Provide Meaningful Opportunities in Work, Family, and Leisure*, New York: A Wiley-Interscience Publication.

Hashimoto, A. (1992), 'Ageing in Japan', in D.R. Phillips (ed), *Ageing in East and South-East Asia*, London: Edward Arnold.

Hashimoto, A. (1993), 'Family Relations in Later Life: A Cross-Cultural Perspective', *Generations*, Winter: pp. 24-6.

Hashimoto, A. and Kendig, H.L. (1992), 'Aging in International Perspective', in H. Kendig, A. Hashimoto and L.C. Coppard (eds), *Family Support for the Elderly: The International Experience*, Oxford: Oxford University Press.

Hatta, T. (1998), '*Teiki-Shakuchi-ken ha Nihon no Juutaku Jijou wo Gun to Yokusuru* [Short-Term Leasehold will Improve Housing Situations in Japan', *The Economist (Japan)*, 28 April: pp. 71-4.

Hayakawa, K. (1979), *Jutaku Binbo Monogatari [Poor Housing Stories]*, Tokyo: Iwanami Shoten.

Hayakawa, K. (1993), *Oi no Sumai Gaku [Theory of Housing for Older People]*, Tokyo: Iwanami Shoten.

Hayakawa, K. (1995), *Anshin Shisou no Sumai Gaku [Housing Studies For Safety and Security]*, Tokyo: Sangokan.

Hayakawa, K. (1997), *Kyojuu Fukushi [Housing and Human Well-being]*, Tokyo: Iwanami Shoten.

Hayakawa, K. and Hirayama, Y. (1991), 'The Impact of the Minkatsu Policy on Japanese Housing and Land Use', *Society and Space*, 9: pp. 151-64.

Hayakawa, K. and Okamoto, Y. (1993), *Kyoju Fukushi no Ronri [Theory of Welfare for Living]*, Tokyo: Tokyo University Press.

Health and Welfare Statistics Association, Japan. (1994), *Trends in National Health, 1994*, Tokyo.

Heidenheimer, A.J., Heclo, H. and Adams, C.T. (1983), *Comparative Public Policy: The Politics of Social Choice in Europe and America*, New York: St. Martin's Press.

Hirayama, Y. and Hayakawa, K. (1995), 'Home Ownership and Family Wealth in Japan', in R. Forrest and A. Murie (eds), *Housing and Family Wealth: Comparative International Perspectives*, London: Routledge.

Hirosima, K. (1987), 'The Living Arrangements and Familial Contacts of the Elderly in Japan', *International Institute for Applied Systems Analysis*, Laxenburg.

Hoglund, J.D. (1985), *Housing for the Elderly*, New York: Van Nostrand Reinhold.

Holden, K.C. (1983), 'Changing employment patterns of women', in D. Plath (ed), *Work and Lifecourse in Japan*, Albany: State University of New York.

ILO. (1982), *Improvements in the Quality of Working Life in Three Japanese Industries*, Geneva: ILO.

Institute of Population Problems, Ministry of Health and Welfare, Japan. (1993), *Future Projection on the Number of Households for Japan*, Tokyo.

Ito, A. and Sonoda, M. (1994), *Kourei Jidai wo Sumau: 2025 nen no Sumai eno Teigen [Living in the Ageing Society: Proposal for Living in 2025]*, Tokyo: Tokyo Insho-kan.

Ito, R. et al. (1994), '*Kourei-sha no Kyojuu Idou wo Kangaeru* [Analysing Older People's Migration]', *Aging*. Summer: pp. 2-9.

Ishii, S, Candice, T. and Klopf, D. (1994), 'Value Differences Among Japanese, Korean, and American College Students', *Otsuma Joshi Daigaku Kiyo*, Bunkei, 26 March: pp. 51-6.

Johnson, N. (1993), 'Welfare Pluralism: Opportunities and Risks', in A. Evers and I. Svetlik (eds), *Balancing Pluralism: New Welfare Mixes in Care for the Elderly*, Aldershot: Avebury.

Jones, C. (1993), 'The Pacific Challenge: Confucian Welfare States', in C. Jones (ed), *New Perspectives on the Welfare State in Europe*, London: Routledge.

Kamada, T. and Sasaki, A. (1990), *Rougo Seikatsu no Kyoudou wo Kangaeru [Thinking of Group Living in Later Life]*, Tokyo: Aoki Shoten.

Kamata, S. (1984), *Japan in the Passing Lane*, London: Unwin.

Kamo, Y. (1988), 'A Note on Elderly Living Arrangements in Japan and the United States', *Research on Aging*, Vol. 10, No. 2, June: pp. 297-305.

Kendig, H. (1989), *Social Change and Family Dependency in Old Age: Perceptions of Japanese Women in Middle Age*, Tokyo: Nihon University, Population Research Institute.

Kose, T. (1990), '*Roujin Kaigo Seisaku to Juu-Kinou no Juusoku* [Policies for Old Age Care and Sufficient Function of Housing]', in Institute of Social Security (ed), *Juutaku Seisaku to Shakai Hoshou [Housing Policy and Social Security]*, Tokyo: Tokyo University Press.

Koyama, T. (1962), *Gendai Kazoku no Kenkyu [Study of Modern Family]*, Tokyo: Kobundo.

Koyano, W. (1996), 'Filial Piety and Intergenerational Solidarity in Japan', *Australian Journal on Ageing*, Vol. 15, No. 2: pp. 51-6.

Langan, M. and Ostner, I. (1991), 'Gender and Welfare: Towards a Comparative Framework', in G. Room (ed), *Towards a European Welfare State?*, Bristol: SAUS Publications.

Laslett, P. and Wall, R. (1972), *Household and Family in Past Time*, Cambridge: Cambridge University Press.

Lawton, L., Silverstein, M. and Bengtson, V. (1994), 'Solidarity Between Generations in Families', in V. Bengtson and R. Harootyan (eds), *Intergenerational Linkages: Hidden Connections in American Society*, New York: Springer Publishing Company.

Lawton, M.P. (1986), 'Human Perspectives on Current and Future Housing', *Housing for Older Adults: Options & Answers*, Washington, DC: National Council on the Aging: pp. 8-16.

Lebra, T.S. (1984), *Japanese Women: Constraints and Fulfillment*, Honolulu: University Press of Hawaii.

Lebra, T. and Sugiyama, T. (1979), 'The Dilemma and Strategies of Aging among Contemporary Japanese Women', *Ethnology*, Vol. 18, No. 1: pp. 337-53.

Lee, H.K. (1987), 'The Japanese Welfare State in Transition', in R. Friedmann, N. Gilbert and M. Sherer (eds), *Modern Welfare States: A Comparative View of Trends and Prospects*, Brighton: Wheatsheaf Books.

Levy, M.J. (1955), 'Contrasting Factors in the Modernization of China and Japan', in S.S. Kuznets, W.E. Moore and J.J. Spengler (eds), *Economic Growth: Brazil, India, Japan*, Durham: Duke University Press.

Levy, M.J., Jr. (1965), 'Aspects of the Analysis of Family Structure', in A. Coale, M. Fallers, M.J. Levy, D.M. Schneider and S.S. Tomkins (eds), *Aspects of the Analysis of Family Structure*, Princeton, NJ: Princeton University Press.

Lewis, J. (1992), 'Gender and the Development of Welfare Regimes', *Journal of European Social Policy*, 2 (3): pp. 159-73.

Maeda, D. (1982), 'Aging and Society', Unpublished Report, Tokyo Metropolitan Institute of Gerontology, July.

Maeda, D. (1993), 'Japan', in E. Palmore (ed), *Developments and Research on Aging; An International Handbook*, Westport, Connecticut: Greenwood Press.

Maeda, D. and Shimizu, Y. (1992), 'Family Support for Elderly People in Japan', in H. Kendig, A. Hashimoto and L. Coppard (eds), *Family Support for the Elderly: The International Experience*, Oxford: Oxford University Press.

Management and Coordination Agency, Japan. (1963), *Juutaku Toukei Chousa [Housing Survey of Japan]*, Tokyo: Statistics Bureau.

Management and Coordination Agency, Japan. (1968), *Juutaku Toukei Chousa [Housing Survey of Japan]*, Tokyo: Statistics Bureau.

Management and Coordination Agency, Japan. (1973), *Juutaku Toukei Chousa [Housing Survey of Japan]*, Tokyo: Statistics Bureau.

Management and Coordination Agency, Japan. (1978), *Juutaku Toukei Chousa [Housing Survey of Japan]*, Tokyo: Statistics Bureau.

Management and Coordination Agency, Japan. (1983), *Juutaku Toukei Chousa [Housing Survey of Japan]*, Tokyo: Statistics Bureau.

Management and Coordination Agency, Japan. (1985), *Kokusei Chousa [Population Census of Japan]*, Tokyo: Bureau of Statistics, 3.

Management and Coordination Agency, Japan. (1986), *International Comparative Survey on the Lives and Perceptions of Elders*, Tokyo: Office for the Aged.

Management and Coordination Agency, Japan. (1988), *Juutaku Toukei Chousa [Housing Survey of Japan]*, Tokyo: Statistics Bureau.

Management and Coordination Agency, Japan. (1989), *Choju-Shakai ni Okeru Danjo-Betsu no Ishiki no Keikou ni Kansuru Chousa [Survey on Gender Attitudes to Ageing Society]*, Tokyo.

Management and Coordination Agency, Japan. (1990), *Kokusei Chousa [Population Census of Japan]*, Tokyo: Bureau of Statistics, 3, 7.

Management and Coordination Agency, Japan. (1993), *Juutaku Toukei Chousa [Housing Survey of Japan]*, Tokyo: Statistics Bureau.

Management and Coordination Agency, Japan. (1995), *Kokusei Chousa [Population Census of Japan]*, Tokyo: Bureau of Statistics, 3.

Management and Coordination Agency, Japan. (1996), *Brief Summary of the Fourth International Comparative Survey of the Elderly*, Tokyo.

Maruo, N. (1986), 'The Development of the Welfare Mix in Japan', in R. Rose and R. Shiratori (eds), *The Welfare State East and West*, Oxford: Oxford University Press.

Maruo, N. (1990), '*Juutaku Seisaku to Fukushi* [Housing Policy and Welfare]', in *Juutaku Seisaku to Shakai Hosho [Housing Policy and Social Security]*, Tokyo: University of Tokyo Press.

Maruo, N. (1992), 'The Impact of the Aging Population on the Social Security and Allied Services of Japan', *Review of Social Policy*, No.1: pp. 1-54.

Masuda, K. (1979), '*Kourei-ka Shakai to Kazoku* [Ageing Society and Family]', in T. Sakata (ed), *Asu no Toshi [A City of Tomorrow]*, Tokyo: Chuo Houki Shuppan.

Matsumoto, Y.S. (1968), 'Contemporary Japan: The Individual and the Group', *Transactions of the American Philosophical Society*, 50, January: pp. 1-75.

Maykovich, M.K. (1978), 'The Japanese Family', in M.S. Das and P.D. Bardis (eds), *Family in Asia*, New Delhi: Vikas Publishing House.

Meguro, Y. (1987), *Kojinka suru Kazoku [Individualizing Family]*, Tokyo: Keisou Shobou.

Meshida, H. (1991), '*Yuuryou Roujin Home: Sono Meishou to Yurai* [Private Housing Development for Older Prople: Its Name and Origin]', *Aging*, Spring: pp. 3-10.

Ministry of Construction, Japan. (1995), *Minkan Juutaku Kensetsu Shikin Jittai Chousa [Survey on the Financial Situation in Private Home Construction]*, Tokyo.

Ministry of Foreign Affairs, Japan. (1995), *Kaigai Zairyuu Houjin-Suu Chousa Toukei [Survey on Numbers of Japanese People in Overseas]*, Tokyo.

Ministry of Health and Welfare, Japan. (1990), *Kousei Hakusho [White Paper on Health and Welfare]*, Tokyo.

Ministry of Health and Welfare, Japan. (1991), *Kokumin Seikatsu Kiso Chousa [Basic Survey on the Life of People in Japan]*, Tokyo.

Ministry of Health and Welfare, Japan. (1992a), *Kokumin Seikatsu Kiso Chousa [Basic Survey on the Life of People in Japan]*, Tokyo.

Ministry of Health and Welfare, Japan. (1992b), *Shakai Fukushi Shisetsu Chousa Houkoku [Survey Report of Social Welfare Housing]*, Tokyo.

Ministry of Health and Welfare, Japan. (1995), *Kousei Hakusho [White Paper on Health and Welfare]*, Tokyo.

Ministry of Transportation, Japan. (1990), *Major City Traffic Census*, Tokyo.

Mishra, R. (1990), *The Welfare State in Capitalist Society: Policies of Retrenchment and Maintenance in Europe, North America and Australia*, London: Harvester Wheatsheaf.

172 *Changing Family and Housing in Post-War Japanese Society*

Miura, F., Imada, T., Naoi, M. and Yoshioka, S. (1995), '*Kourei-Sha Hitori-Gurashi / Fuufu-Setai ni Kansuru Chousa Kekka Kara* [Analysis of Survey Results on Elderly-Only Households]', *Aging*, Winter: pp. 2-10.

Miyajima, H. (1997), *Kourei-Shakai heno Message [Messages for the Ageing Society]*, Tokyo: Maruzen.

Morgan, S.P. and Hirosima, K. (1983), 'The Persistence of Extended Family Residence in Japan: Anachronism or Alternative Strategy?', *American Sociological Review*, Vol. 48, No. 2: pp. 269-81.

Mori, H. (1995), 'Structural Changes in Japan's Labour Market and its Attraction of Foreign Migrant Workers', *Journal of International Economic Studies*, 9: pp. 41-66.

Morioka, K. (1973), *Kazoku Shuki-Ron [Family Life Cycle]*, Tokyo: Baifukan.

Morishima, M. (1988), 'Confucianism as a Basis for Capitalism', in D.I. Okimoto and T.P. Rohlem (eds), *Inside the Japanese System: Readings on Contemporary Society and Political Economy*, Stanford: Stanford University Press.

Nakagawa, Y. (1979), 'Japan, the Welfare Super-Power', *The Journal of Japanese Studies*, Vol. 5, No. 1: pp. 5-51.

Nakane, C. (1972) 'An Interpretation of the Size and Structure of the Household in Japan over Three Centuries', in P. Laslett and R. Wall (eds), *Household and Family in Past Time*, London: Cambridge University Press.

Nakane, C. (1974) 'Criteria of Group Formation', in T.S. Lebra and W.P. Lebra (eds), *Japanese Culture and Behavior: Selected Readings*, Honolulu: University of Hawaii Press.

Nasu, S. and Yazawa, Y. (eds) (1973), *Study on Support for the Aged*, Tokyo: Kakiuchi Shuppan.

Nihon Chingin Kenkyu Centre (Japan Income Research Centre). (1985), *Shunki Chingin Koushou Shiryou [Spring Wage Negotiation Data]*, Tokyo.

OECD. (1990), *Health Care Systems in Transition: The Search for Efficiency*, OECD Social Policy Studies, No. 7. Paris: Organization for Economic Co-operation and Development.

Office of the Prime Minister, Japan. (1970), *Kokusei Chousa [Population Census of Japan]*, Tokyo: Bureau of Statistics, 3 and 7.

Office of the Prime Minister, Japan. (1975), *Kokusei Chousa [Population Census of Japan]*, Tokyo: Bureau of Statistics, 3.

Office of the Prime Minister, Japan. (1980), *Kokusei Chousa [Population Census of Japan]*, Tokyo: Bureau of Statistics, 3 and 7.

Office of the Prime Minister, Japan. (1987), *Japan Statistical Yearbook*, Tokyo: Bureau of Statistics.

Office of the Prime Minister, Juvenile Headquarters, Japan. (1994), *Sekaino Seinen tono Hikaku kara Mita Nihon no Seinen [Japanese Youth in Comparison with Youths around the World]*, Tokyo: Ministry of Finance.

Ogawa, N. (1986), 'Internal Migration in Japanese Post-war Development', NUPRI Research Papaer Series, No. 33. Tokyo: Nihon University Population Research Institute.

Ogawa, N. (1992), 'Resources for the Elderly in Economic Development',in H. Kendig, A. Hashimoto and L. Coppard (eds), *Family Support for the Elderly: The International Experience*, Oxford: Oxford University Press.

Ogawa, N and Retherford, R.D. (1997), 'Shifting Costs of Caring for the Elderly Back to Families in Japan: Will It Work?', *Population and Development Review*, 23 (1) March: pp. 59-94.

Ohama, H. (1953), '*Kaji Jigen kara Mita Kazoku no Tenshon* [Family Tension as Viewed from Domestic Cases]', in Nihon Jimbun Kagaku-kai (ed), *Shakaiteki Kincho no Kenkyu [Studies in Social Tension]*, Tokyo: Yuhikaku.

Ohashi, K. and Masuda, K. (1968), *Kazoku Shakaigaku [Family Sociology]*, Tokyo: Kawashima Shoten.

Ohmoto, K. (1996), '*Kyojuu Seisaku no Gendai-shi* [History of Policies for Human Settlement]', in *Kouza Gendai Kyojuu: 1. Rekishi to Shisou [Human Settlement and the Right to Housing in Japan: 1. History and Philosophy]*, Tokyo: Tokyo University Press.

Oizumi, E. (1994), 'Property Finance in Japan: Expansion and Collapse of the Bubble Economy', *Environment and Planning*, Vol. 26: pp. 199-213.

Okamoto, T. (1996), 'Welfare for the Elderly in Japan', in *Decline of Fertility and Population Aging in East Asia*, Tokyo: International Longevity Center.

Okamoto, Y., Sato, S., Hada, S., Arai, A. and Hashimoto, H. (1993), '*Kourei-Shakai to Zaitaku Care* [The Ageing Society and Domicility Care]', *Jurist*, April: pp. 2-12.

Okazaki, Y. (1991), '*Kourei-ka Shakai to Kazoku no Mondai* [Issues of Ageing Society and Family]', *Aging*, Autumn: pp. 4-8.

Oouchi, H. et al. (1971), *Illustrated Japanese Economy* (5th Edition), Tokyo: Iwanami Shoten.

Osawa, M. (1993), *Kigyo Chuushin Shakai wo Koete: Gendai Nihon wo Gender de Yomu [Beyond the Firm-Oriented Society: Examine Modern Japan with Gender Studies]*, Tokyo: Jiji Press.

Palmore, E.B. and Maeda, D. (1985), *The Honorable Elders Revisited*, Durham: Duke University Press.

Patrick, H.T. and Rohlen, T.P. (1987), 'Small-Scale Family Enterprises', *The Political Economy of Japan Vol. 1: The Domestic Transformation*, Stanford: Stanford University Press.

Plath, D. (1972), 'Japan: The After Years', in D. Cowgill and L. Holmes (eds), *Aging and Modernization*, New York: Appleton-Century-Crofts.

Pynoos, J. and Liebig, P.S. (1995), 'Housing Policy for Frail Elders: Trends and Implications for Long-Term Care', in J. Pynoos and P. Liebig (eds), *Housing Frail Elders: International Policies, Perspectives, and Prospects*, Baltimore: Johns Hopkins University Press.

Rein, M. and Rainwater, L. (1986), 'Introduction', in M. Rein and L. Rainwater (eds), *Public / Private Interplay in Social Protection*, New York: M.E. Sharpe.

Reischauer, W. (1977), *The Japanese*, Cambridge, MA: Harvard University Press.

Rice, J.J. and Bain, W.C. (1986), 'Keeping the Elderly in Existing Communities: The Hamilton East Kiwanis Non-Profit Housing Program', in G. Gutman and N. Blackie (eds), *Aging in Place: Housing Adaptations and Options for Remaining in the Community*, Burnaby: Gerontology Research Center, Simon Fraser University.

Riley, M.W., Kahn, R.L. and Foner, A. (eds) (1994), *Age and Structural Lag: Society's Failure to Provide Meaningful Opportunities in Work, Family, and Leisure*, New York: A Wiley-Interscience Publication.

Rose, R. (1986), 'Common Goals but Different Roles: The State's Contribution to the Welfare Mix', in R. Rose and R. Shiratori (eds), *The Welfare State East and West*, Oxford: Oxford University Press.

Rose, R and Shiratori, R. (1986), 'Introduction: Welfare in Society: Three Worlds or One?', in R. Rose and R. Shiratori (eds), *The Welfare State East and West*, Oxford: Oxford University Press.

Rozman, G. (1992), 'The Confucian Faces of Capitalism', in M. Borthwick (ed) *Pacific Century: The Emergence of Modern Pacific Asia*, Boulder: Westview.

Rudd, C. (1994), 'Japan's Welfare Mix', *The Japan Foundation Newsletter*, Vol. 22, No.3: pp. 14-7.

Sano, C. (1958), 'Changing Values of the Japanese Family', *Anthropological Series*, 18. Washington, DC: Catholic University of America.

Schaede, U. (1996), 'Economy', *Regional Surveys of the World: The Far East & Australasia* (26th Edition), London: Europa Publications.

Sellek, Y. (1997), '*Nikkeijin*: The Phenomenon of Return Migration', in M. Weiner (ed), *Japan's Minorities: The Illusion of Homogeneity*, London: Routledge.

Sellek, Y. and Weiner, M.A. (1992), 'Migrant Workers: the Japanese Case in International Perspective', in G.D. Hook and M.A. Weiner (eds), *The Internationalization of Japan*, London: Routledge.

Shiratori, R. (1986), 'The Future of the Welfare State', in R. Rose and R. Shiratori (eds), *The Welfare State East and West*, Oxford: Oxford University Press.

Shouji, Y. (1993), '*Gendai Kazoku no Kaigo-ryoku: Kitai, Genjitsu, Tenbou* [The modern family's ability of old-age care: expectation, reality, and perspectives]', *Jurist*, April: pp. 190-96.

Sugimoto, Y. (1997), *An Introduction to Japanese Society*, Cambridge: Cambridge University Press.

Sussman, M.B., Romeis, J.C. and Maeda, D. (1980), 'Age Bias in Japan: Implications for Normative Conflict', *International Review of Modern Sociology*, No. 10: pp. 243-54.

Suzuki, Y. (1989), *San-Sedai Doukyo: Koufuku na Doukyo ha Kanou ka [Three Generational Living: Is it Possible to Live Happily with Other Generations]*, Tokyo: Yuhikaku.

Svetlik, I. (1993), 'Regulation of the Plural and Mixed Welfare System', in A. Evers and I. Svetlik (eds), *Balancing Pluralism: New Welfare Mixes in Care for the Elderly*, Aldershot: Avebury.

Tabata, H. (1990), 'The Japanese Welfare State: Its Structure and Transformation', *The Annals of the Institute of Social Science*, No. 32 4. University of Tokyo.

Takahashi, T. and Someya, Y. (1985), 'Japan', in J. Dixon and H.S. Kim (eds), *Social Welfare in Asia*, London: Croom Helm.

Takenaka, E. (1996), '*Danjo Kyousei Shakai no Shakai Hoshou wo Kangaeru Kihon Shiten* [Basic Viewpoint on Social Security System towards Gender Equal Society]', in Kansai Onna no Roudou Mondai Kenkyu-kai (ed), *Danjo Kyousei Shakai no Shakai Hoshou Vision*, Tokyo: Domes Shuppan.

Taylor-Gooby, P. (1991), 'Welfare State Regimes and Welfare Citizenship', *Journal of European Social Policy*, 1 (2): pp. 93-105.

Titmuss, R.M. (1963), 'The Social Division of Welfare', *Essays on the Welfare State*, London: Allen and Unwin.

Tsuru, S. (1993), *Japan's Capitalism: Creative Defeat and Beyond*, Cambridge: Cambridge University Press.

US Bureau of the Census. (1987), *An Aging World*, International Population Reports, Washington DC: US Government Printing Office.

US Bureau of the Census. (1993), *An Aging World II*, International Population Reports, Washington DC: US Government Printing Office.

US Bureau of the Census. (1996), *Global Aging in to the 21st Century*, Washington DC: US Government Printing Office.

Vogel, E.F. (1965), 'The Japanese Family', in M.F. Nimkoff (ed), *Comparative Family Systems*, Boston: Houghton Mifflin Company.

Yasukochi, K. (1995), 'Support Problems in the Aging Urban Society', *Review of Social Policy*, March: pp. 43-64.

Yazawa, S. (ed) (1993), *Toshi to Josei no Shakaigaku [Sociology of City and Women: Beyond Collapse of Division of Labour by Gender]*, Tokyo: Science-sha.

Yoshida, K. (1993), '*Kourei Josei no Seikatsu Jittai* [Lives of Older women]', in M. Miyamoto (ed), *Kourei-ka to Kazoku no Shakai-gaku [Sociology of Ageing and the Family]*, Tokyo: Bunka Shobou Hakubun-sha.

Yoshizaki, Y. (1997), 'The Value Shift of Japanese Youth', *Comparative Civilizations Review*, No. 35 Winter: pp. 1-14.

Zenkoku Shakai Fukushi Kyougikai (Social Welfare Council). (1994), *Kourei-sha Hakusho [White Paper on Ageing]*, F. Miura (ed), Tokyo.

Appendix A

Methodology and Approach

Fieldwork

A qualitative approach was mainly used for the fieldwork research with a series of semi-structured, in-depth interviews with 29 older Japanese women. Further interviews were carried out with middle-aged women, local government officers (e.g. The Housing Department and The Health and Welfare Department), policy implementors and service providers for older people (e.g. public health nurses), and wardens of the housing schemes for older people to supplement the interviews conducted with the older women. Those interviews with the professionals were planned to contextualize the interviews with older women, and also to assist the evaluation of the results and findings of the household research. Although one focus group interview with seven middle-aged women was also conducted in the later stage of the fieldwork, the data were only used as an additional sensitizing device to illustrate the significance of issues and the future direction of the ageing society.

All interviews were arranged in advance. The prospective older informants were identified through purposive selection, and contacted initially through key informants such as civil servants, a warden of homes, public health nurses and community workers. A snowballing technique was also applied in order to expand access to potential older informants. A letter followed the initial contact introducing the purpose of the research, its confidentiality and voluntary nature, and its outcome. All interviews with older people were planned to take place in their own home, which would allow the researcher to observe their dwellings and to create a relatively informal atmosphere. Two interviews were, however, held in the communal lounge of a housing development, and another two in a spare room in a clinic. A few people were reluctant to invite the researcher into their house because of the inconvenience or perceived embarrassment due to dwelling size or state of tidiness. The style of the interviews was semi-structured and avoided a formal questionnaire approach. Each informant was interviewed for an hour to an hour-and-a-half on average. All interviews were taperecorded with the informants' consent, and all tapes were summarized in Japanese in order not to lose the original meanings.

The following criteria were set in advance in order to cover targeted groups of older people:

• *Gender: female only.* Issues of an ageing society were often issues of older women because higher proportions of the older population were female (60% in the city in 1990); due to the higher longevity of females (82.8 years for women compared with 76.4 years for men in 1995); the age group was likely to be widowed (10% of men but 44% of women aged 60 years and over are widowed in Japan (US Bureau of the Census, 1996)); and women were also likely to be disadvantaged by the prevailing political and economic systems. As a result of a male-dominated society in Japan, women experienced particular difficulties and inequalities, especially when they became older.

• *Age: between 70 and 79 years old.* Older women in this cohort had all experienced a common set of post-war legal, economic and social changes. The analysis, however, included some women aged 80 or over who were able to contribute relevant or valuable information.

• *Marital status: without a spouse.* The research targeted women who had been married and had children, but who had become single through either widowhood or divorce. Although this filter was thought to eliminate husband and wife relationships from the analysis, some informants illustrated how their lives changed dramatically with the death of their spouse. People tended to hold different views and attitudes towards housing choices and relations with their adult children depending on their marital status. The research, however, included two never-married women.

• *Family composition: must have children.* The research focused on the transformation of intergenerational relations.   However, two never-married women who had alternative means of family support by other relatives (e.g. sisters, a nephew) were included.

- *Living arrangement.* Ten informants were selected from people who were living with their adult children. The coresidents had to be members of the same family, most commonly a son and his family, or a daughter and her family. The other 19 informants were chosen from single-elderly households who were either living on their own in a private house or living in a group home.

- *Housing/welfare sectors.* In order to examine the issues affecting older women in different housing settings, three welfare sectors (the family, the market and the state) were identified. It helped to make a clear distinction among older women in terms of their socio-economic status, tenure and dwelling type, living arrangement, or degree of inter-generational solidarity. Between 10 and 12 informants were interviewed from each welfare sector (including four pilot interviews):

  > *The family.* The most important criterion in the family sector was living with their adult children. In order to have a variety of informants, other cases besides a traditional coresidency case (such as a widow living with her married first son in her own single-family home) were also included. For example, a widow living with her married daughter, with her son-in-law, or with her unmarried children in rented housing were all approached for interview. Besides having a range of a household compositions, the timing of starting coresidency also needed to be considered. The research included both cases where adult children had never left their parents' home, and where a parent and adult children had started living together when a change in their circumstances occurred (e.g. a spouse's death, retirement).

  > *The market.* Selection in the market sector targeted mainly older women who were relatively well-off; those who lived independently in their own house; and those who moved into one of the private purpose-built retirement flats in the city.
  >
  > Four residents in a private purpose-built retirement flat were approached for interview. All of them belonged to a higher

socio-economic group. This particular housing development in the city was opened in 1988, in response to new demands during the bubble economy period. One of the three multi-storey buildings was an owner-occupied condominium; and units of the other two buildings were sold as 'life-estate', which was introduced as an alternative to new private housing developments for older people. The buildings were located in a convenient area: close to shops, medical services, and banks, with good access to public transportation. The buildings were designed barrier-free with special features and facilities (e.g. an emergency alarm, a big common bath, a lounge and activity rooms), and provided some support services (e.g. three hot meals a day in a dining room, 24-hour reception service and arranged social activities). The development was linked to a major hospital in the city but no on-site medical services, apart from regular health checks, were offered.

Investigating reasons why those women chose or were forced to live independently from their adult children was another key research objective. The research, therefore, included older women whose adult children were living both nearby and at a distance. In addition, the research explored the case of single-elderly renters, a small group but significant in policy terms. One female renter on low income who received no benefit beside her pension was interviewed, along with some women who had considered renting. The research interest in the renter group was predominantly concerned with how they could secure their old age without their own house and to analyse the availability and affordability of the rental market for such individuals.

The state. People living in state sector housing were selected for interview as representatives of a lower socio-economic group. Two housing projects both funded by the local authority were chosen for the purpose of the research.

Residents in *Itawari Juutaku*, or Silver Housing, were approached for interview. It is purpose-built rental housing for older people, funded and operated by the local authority as a pilot project under new national guidelines. Some support services, such as a live-in warden called a life-support advisor (LSA), were unique features of the development. This particular development was opened in 1993, and was located in the least convenient area of the city as part of a large-scale public housing development. The majority of the units are barrier-free 1DK (one-bedroom unit with an adjoined dining kitchen and a unit bathroom), although some two-bedroom units are also available. Apart from having a LSA and a common room, not many differences distinguished these units from ordinary rental housing. The monthly rent for a single-occupancy unit in 1996 was around ¥27,000 (£135). The residents were required to be over 60 years old, physically independent, and have an income in a certain range. In 1996, 70% of the residents were female, and the average age was 75 years old. This project is likely to remain as a model project in the city, rather than as a starting point for further development, due to the limited financial resources of the local authority. Little assessment seems to have been made in terms of the project's overall design and operation.

For the second housing project, some residents in *yougo roujin home*, a home for older people, were interviewed. In Japan, this type of publicly-funded group home for older people tends to be translated into English as a 'nursing' home, although extensive nursing care is not provided. This particular home was opened in 1956 and its role and facilities were redefined in 1973. To be eligible for the unit, residents had to be over 65 years old, and have difficulty in maintaining their life for health, social, or financial reasons in ordinary dwellings. Since one criterion specified the ability to carry out daily tasks, the main reason for the residents' dependency on the state was financial. The duties of the manager and the staff in the home included helping the residents to structure their daily life with routine activities as well as social clubs and events. In 1997, almost all the 80 residents lived in private rooms (4.5 *tatami*-mat room [equivalent to 7.29m^2]) with a toilet shared between two residents. Even such a small room (without a private bathroom) was a relative luxury for an average home, since a shared room with two to four people was still a common arrangement.

In addition, older women living alone in subsidized public housing or rental housing on state benefit (housing allowance) were included. Two women who were 'socially hospitalized' were also approached for interview.

Ethical, Logistical, and Practical Considerations

The research revealed that many older women were 'willing to talk'. Since people tend to experience loneliness and isolation when they become older, the majority of the women welcomed an opportunity to talk to other people (Finch, 1993). There was only one extreme case where an informant was reluctant to be interviewed at the beginning. In Japan, culturally and socially, people are not accustomed to expressing their feelings, problems, or personal concerns openly and freely among family and friends, or in schools and workplaces. In addition, due to the tendency of having two different sets of values called *honne* [real, personal motives for daily life] and *tatemae* [identification with normative patterns of society] (Benedict, 1947), getting true and honest responses from informants was indeed challenging. A qualitative approach helped to reach the older women's *honne*, and succeeded in illustrating and analysing their experiences within the theoretical framework set for the research. An underdeveloped counselling system may be another reason why opportunities to talk about themselves were limited. Seeking professional help for emotional or psychological distress (or simply wanting companionship for loneliness) has not been a socially acceptable option for any age group in Japan. For many people, it can be seen as a shame or stigma, and may present a loss of face (and respect) in public. Talking to a stranger seemed, however, less threatening for the older women to disclose their stories. Under such circumstances, the opportunity of being interviewed was surprisingly welcomed by many women. The majority were eager to talk about their personal history, often in detail and with occasional tears. At the end of the interview, the women were often very appreciative that the researcher had come to listen to them, and frequently apologized for relating too many *tsumaranai* [unimportant] stories for too long. The following comment and telephone call illustrate their experience of being interviewed:

> "*It was so refreshing to talk to you. I didn't realize how quickly time went by. After my husband died, there was no guest visited me. [Talking to you was] as if a light beamed into my dull and routine life.*"

One informant telephoned the researcher the following morning of the interview. "*Can I have the interview tape when you finish it? ...No, I'm not worrying about the confidentiality or misuse of the tape. Actually, I had never told anyone of my family the stories which I told you in the interview. That's why I want to leave the tape to my daughters and*

> *grand-sons.   Then, they can listen to my past and my feelings after my death."*

Scheduling interviews with older women was relatively easy, since they usually had no commitment to paid work and much less commitment to family duties compared with the younger age groups.   Due to their availability, most of the interviews were scheduled and conducted at short notice, usually for the following day from an initial contact.   Occasionally, the scheduling process went on very quickly – one interview took place within one hour from an initial telephone contact.   That informant then introduced another woman living nearby, who was interviewed right after the first interview.   Moreover, including a clinic as a key informant (contact source) expanded the choice of older informants substantially.   This raised the issue of social hospitalization, and illustrated case histories for some of the older women.

There were some potential shortcomings in the selection process. For example, if informants were from the same neighbourhood, they were likely to be of a similar socio-economic status.   Therefore, the research chose a range of neighbourhoods to select older informants.   In addition, if one key informant introduced some older informants, these may have shared similar opinions.   Even though they were introduced by the same key informant, however, the research found that background, living situations, and views of older informants varied quite widely.

Having wardens and housing managers as key informants (contact sources) to gain access to the residents of three housing developments aided the research.   Since the managers held a data file of all the residents, the selection process was made more effective by targeting older informants according to the pre-defined criteria.   However, one consideration remained in that the managers inevitably screened the potential informants, which may have created a bias towards the selection.   They tended to introduce the researcher to someone approachable, positive, and able to 'talk' coherently to cover the research purpose.   By the same token, some women refused to participate in the research when they were experiencing economic hardship or family problems.

Interviewing family members of older informants was thought to serve the useful purpose of cross-validation.   Since older people in general have a 'yes tendency,' obtaining their *honne* [real opinion] and factual-based views were assumed to be challenging from the outset (Miura et al, 1995). A less biased and more complete picture of each informant was also possible to be gained through interviewing their family members, neighbours, or wardens of housing developments. However, the majority of the older women were willing to talk and were remarkably open about themselves to the researcher. Given the fact that some women admitted that it was easier to talk to the researcher than to the family, the purpose of cross-validation did not become a priority in the research.

Appendix B

Glossary

B

bakufu
military government under *shogun* (e.g. Kamakura *bakufu* [1192-1333], and Tokugawa [*Edo*] *bakufu* [1603-1867])

butsudan
a Buddhist alter for the home, in which mortuary tables of one's ancestors are placed (see *hotoke*)

C

chien
blood relations

chien
community ties

D

doukyo
living intergenerationally between older parents and their adult children

duskin
chemical mop

E

enryo
reservation, hesitation

F

fukoku kyouhei
'rich nation, strong army'; the national slogan in the *Meiji* period

fukushi gannen
'welfare year one'; the national slogan in 1973 to emphasise state priority from economic growth to welfare

G

gimu   obligation, to repay limitless indebtedness
giri   obligation; also used as term for in-laws

H

haka   tomb
honne   real, personal motives for daily life (see also
                     tatemae)
hotoke   ancestors; also implies as *butsudan*

I

ie   family, household, lineage, home, or house: the *Ie*
                     system [the family system (lineage which is
                     conceptualized as continuously succeeding from
                     generation to generation)]
ikigai   meaning of life

J

juku   cramming classes held outside normal school hours

K

kafuu   family traditions and customs
kanreki   the sixty-first year after birth, literally the
                     commencement of a new cycle in the Chinese
                     calendar
kigyou-senshi   corporate warrior
kiken   dangerous
kitanai   dirty
kitsui   difficult
koudan juutaku   subsidized rental housing provided by the Housing
                     Corporation

M

manshon   medium to high-rise condominiums for purchase

N

nenkou-joretsu   seniority system in the workplace (e.g. promotion
                     and income)
nihon-gata fukushi 'Japanese style welfare society'

nikkeijin   descendants of Japanese immigrants (e.g. South-
                                   American-Japanese)
ni-setai juutaku   two-household housing
niwa-tsuki ikko-date   a single-family home with private garden

O
on   a debt of gratitude, an obligation (e.g. the debt
                                   children owe their parents for having suffered and
                                   sacrificed throughout their children's upbringing)
onna wa sankai ni Ie nasi
                                   once women were married, there was no other
                                   home to go back to but their husband's'
oubei ni, oitsuke, oikose
                                   catch up and overtake Europe and America';
                                   the national slogan in the late 1960s
oya-koukou   filial piety, the absolute duty to parents

P
paat   part-time workers; or workers working the same
                                   hours as full-time employees, but in a temporary
                                   status without social security benefits or
                                   contributions

R
roujin   older people: e.g. *roujin mondai* [an issue for older
                                   people]

S
sakoku   the isolation policy of the *Edo* period
sekentei   appearance to the public
shaen   company-based ties
shiei juutaku   public housing for rental
shogun   general (= leader)
shufu   housewife
shuushin-koyou   life-time employment system

T
tanshin-funin   proceeding to a new post without one's family
                                   (company-related transfer)

tanin	non-family, strangers, or non-blood related 'other' people
tatemae	identification with normative patterns of society (see also *honne*)
tateru	to build (e.g. *ie wo tateru* [building a house])
tateuri juutaku	built-for-sale housing
tenkinzoku	transferable employees
tsumaranai	unimportant

Y

yome	a bride of the family (under the *Ie* system)
yougo roujin home	a public home for older people
youshi	man who marries and takes his wife's surname, and succeeds her household (↔ *yome*)
yourouin	pre-war public nursing homes for older people